Orchard Recipes from Eastern England

Orchard Recipes from Eastern England

landscape, fruit and heritage

Monica Askay and Tom Williamson

Copyright © Monica Askay and Tom Williamson.

This edition 2020 published by Bridge Publishing, Lowestoft, NR32 3BB.

Bridge Publishing is an imprint of Poppyland Publishing.

www.poppyland.co.uk

ISBN 978 1 869831 32 5

Designed and typeset in 10.5 on 13.5 pt Gilamesh Pro.

Printed by Ashford Colour Press.

Front cover: Greengages gained their English name from the Gage family of Hengrave Hall in Suffolk.

Contents

Recipes

Acknowledgements

Many people have helped us in producing this book. We would like to thank, in particular, Gerry Barnes, Peter Brears, Gen Broad, Rowena Burgess, Colin Carpenter, Barry Chevallier, Stephen Coleman, Patsy Dallas, Jon Gregory, Martin Hicks, Howard Jones, Peter Laws, Bob Lever, Steve Oram, Paul Read, Margaret Roberts, Rachel Savage, Martin Skipper, Sally Wileman and Clara Zwetsloot. Thanks also to the staff of the Bedfordshire Archives and Records Service; the Cambridgeshire Record Office; the Cambridgeshire Collection; Essex Record Office; Hertfordshire Archives and Local Studies; Norfolk Record Office; the Suffolk Record Offices at Bury St Edmunds and Ipswich; and Tiptree Jam Museum.

Thanks to Hertfordshire Archives and Local Studies for permission to reproduce Figure 2.2; Dacorum Borough Council, for Figure 2.3; Bedfordshire Archives and Records Service, for Figures 3.4 and 3.5; Tiptree Jam Museum, for Figure 4.2; Gerry Barnes, for Figure 4.5; Norfolk Record Office for Figure 5.4; Attleborough Heritage Centre, for Figure 5.7; Girton College, for Figure 7.3; Alamy photos, for Figure 7.4. Figures 2.10, 3.9, 3.10, 3.11, 4.6, 4.8, 5.8, 5.9, 5.10, 6.6, 6.9, 7.6, 7.7 and 7.9 are all by Daniel Jones; 2.11, 2.12, 4.7, 6.7, 6.8 and 7.9 are by Paul Read; and 1.3 by Bob Lever.

The maps were created from GIS layers provided by the various county environmental records centres: our thanks, in particular, to Phil Ricketts, Ian Carle, Jackie Ulyett, Sam Neal, Lorna Shore and Colin Sanford, together with their teams.

This book is one of the outcomes of 'Orchards East', a project supported by the Heritage Fund, which also provided the resources without which it could not have been published.

Lane's Prince Albert, probably the most famous of Hertfordshire's apple varieties.

Introduction
A Land of Orchards

TODAY, when we think of fruit growing, images of the cherry orchards of Kent or the cider orchards of the West Midlands and the West Country come to mind. But the orchards of the eastern counties also have a long and important history, albeit one often overlooked. Until very recently, orchards were a common sight in the region, a familiar part of the landscape. Some were associated with farmhouses and were filled with tall, spreading trees (Figure 1.1). Others were old commercial enterprises, established in the first half of the twentieth century, or were planted close to hospitals, colleges or other institutions to provide food for the residents. Many were intensively-managed fruit farms, with low-growing trees, closely spaced. Whatever their precise type, since the 1970s numbers have fallen, for a variety of reasons: the rise of the great supermarket chains, increasing levels of foreign imports, the decline of small farms, changes in agricultural subsidies and, perhaps most importantly, changes in lifestyles and in our attitudes to food.

1.1 A traditional farm orchard in Norfolk, with old trees on vigorous rootstocks.

1

Not only have we lost the majority of our orchards. Over the decades the range of fruit varieties grown in the eastern counties, as in the country as a whole, has steadily dwindled. Until quite recently many kinds of apple, and of other fruit, were cultivated in the region and were available for purchase. Most shops now only sell a limited number, many with recent origins. This is not simply a matter of losing some odd-looking fruit with strange, evocative names—D'Arcy Spice, Dr Harvey, Norfolk Beefing (Figure 1.2). It also means that a diverse range of tastes has disappeared from our experience, almost without us noticing.

This short book looks at the history of orchards in eastern England, and of the fruit grown within them. But it is also a recipe book, which provides examples of how different kinds of fruit typical of the eastern counties—varieties of apple, pear, plum and cherry—can be used and eaten. We present a mixture of historic recipes, long-established 'traditional' recipes, and also new ones specially devised to make the best use of the fruit most closely associated with the old counties of Hertfordshire, Bedfordshire, Essex, Norfolk, Suffolk and Cambridgeshire.

1.2 *The Norfolk Beefing, an old culinary apple, first recorded in 1698.*

The conservation of old orchards, and the perpetuation of old varieties, are intimately connected with culinary practices. Many types of fruit can only be eaten with pleasure if used or prepared in the correct ways, and when they are at their seasonal peak. Indeed, different varieties—of apple especially—were intended to fulfil particular functions. Some were ready for picking early in the season, others late; some were for immediate consumption, some could be stored for months. Some were 'eaters' or 'dessert' fruit, consumed raw, but others were 'culinary', and intended for particular types of cooking. Some apples (often referred to as 'codlins') are reduced on cooking to a smooth mush, while others hold their shape well. Some are good for pies, some for toffee apples.

As many readers will be aware, new fruit trees are usually created by a process known as 'grafting'. Pieces of 'scion wood'—small sticks—are cut from a tree of a desired type and carefully spliced onto a dependable 'root stock'. This is because most domesticated fruit will not 'breed true'. If we take a pip from, say, a Cox's Orange Pippin and plant it in the soil it will not grow into a Cox's tree. Every pip will represent a new genetic variation. Only by grafting wood from an existing

Cox's tree, onto a rootstock, can a new tree of this variety be obtained. Most of the chance variations arising from sown pips will be hard, bitter, or at best bland. But some seedling trees, growing by chance from discarded fruit, will produce new apples which are attractive and useful, and will therefore be chosen for grafting and propagation, and then sold by commercial nurseries. New varieties also emerge from 'sports', that is, as a genetic mutation arising on the tree itself—as a branch bearing fruit (and sometimes leaves) different from those on the rest of the tree. Once again, if the new fruit had appealing qualities, a cutting might be taken and grafted, and a new variety thus developed. But in addition to the emergence of new varieties by chance in these ways, fruit breeders also deliberately developed novel types, by cross-pollinating established varieties with desirable characteristics.

Rootstocks come in a variety of forms. In the case of apples, early writers made a distinction between 'crab' or 'wilding' stocks, and 'paradise'. The former produced tall, vigorous, spreading trees; the latter, dwarfing or semi-dwarfing specimens. During the twentieth century a range of improved, more disease-resistant rootstocks was developed at the East Malling Research Station in Kent, some in conjunction with the John Innes Institute, then based in Merton. Many of these rootstocks remain in use. Amongst the most popular are 'MM 106' and 'M25', which produce small, 'dwarf' trees, and tall vigorous ones, respectively. Having said this, the 'vigour' of a tree—how fast and how tall it grows—is the consequence of both rootstock type and of the variety of the graft. Bramley's Seedling, for example, for many decades our most popular cooking apple, always towers above neighbouring trees in an orchard, even when these are grafted onto the same kind of rootstock—unless grown as half standards, as was the custom in the Fens, and even then they develop surprisingly large trunks (Figure 1.3). Pears, which often grow much taller than apples, were originally grafted onto wild pear stock, but from at least the nineteenth century onto rootstocks of quince. Most cherries, plums and other fruit are similarly grafted, on rootstocks selected for their suitability for the location in question, although some, such as greengages, can be grown almost 'true' from seed. One other distinctive feature, of apples in particular, needs to be noted. An orchard planted with a single variety of apple trees will not usually produce much, if any, fruit. Although some types of apple are self-fertile, most need pollen from another variety which comes into blossom at the

1.3 A massive half-standard Bramley's Seedling apple tree in an orchard at Upwell in Norfolk.

same time and even self-fertile varieties generally do better in the presence of a compatible partner.

Some of the varieties of fruit discussed in this book are ancient. Their origins are lost in the mists of time. But many others, as we shall see, originated in the course of the eighteenth, nineteenth or twentieth centuries. Most began by chance, growing from discarded stones or pips or as 'sports' which were then propagated and marketed by local nurseries. While most of these varieties can be found throughout eastern England, many are closely associated with just one county or district. Moreover, particular areas—because of their soils, climate or access to markets—often came to specialise in particular types of fruit. Cherries were the main produce, from an early date, of the west Hertfordshire orchards; a distinctive variety of damson called the 'Aylesbury Prune' was grown in a limited area of south Bedfordshire. Some areas of eastern England were thus, by the eighteenth or nineteenth centuries, particularly concerned with fruit growing, and here orchards were thick on the ground. In others, by contrast, fruit production never came to be a major activity, and orchards remained small and scattered. In all these ways, and others, the character of orchards was intimately connected with other aspects of local and regional history—economic, social and culinary. Orchards were woven into the fabric of local life, and their presence both encouraged, and might be stimulated by, particular local industries, such as cider making or jam production.

The Ordnance Survey 6-inch maps, surveyed around 1900, show that orchards were strongly clustered in a number of key areas of eastern England (Figure 1.4: the counties shown are the 'traditional' ones, with their nineteenth-century boundaries, so that Cambridgeshire excludes Huntingdonshire). Orchards were numerous in the district around Wisbech in the Fenland, straddling the border between Norfolk and Cambridgeshire, and in the centre and south of the latter county. There were also significant concentrations in south Bedfordshire; in west and, to an extent, south-east Hertfordshire; and in the district around Southend in south-east Essex. Although fruit growing was to expand significantly over following decades, these were to remain the main centres of production. The more general scatter of sites across the region which existed in 1900, as shown in Figure 1.4, mostly represent small farm orchards, mainly although not entirely producing fruit for domestic consumption, as well as orchards attached to country houses and to institutions like hospitals.

The areas of large-scale commercial production developed, as we shall see, in various ways and at various times. To some extent, specialisation was influenced by the nature of the local soils. In particular, commercial growers

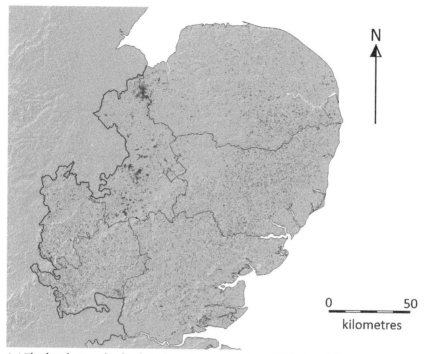

1.4 *The distribution of orchards in the eastern counties in c. 1900, plotted from contemporary Ordnance Survey maps. The counties shown are the 'traditional' ones, with boundaries as they were in the nineteenth century: Cambridgeshire thus excludes the county of Huntingdonshire.*

tended to avoid poorly-draining clays—apples and cherries in particular do not flourish where soils are subject to seasonal waterlogging. Conversely, they also avoided thin, dry and especially acidic soils, locations where trees would have insufficient water during the summer months to grow well and provide a good crop in the autumn. One writer explained in 1924, that while it was difficult to establish fruit trees in chalk, it was worth looking for orchard sites 'in the neighbourhood of chalk'. By this he meant places where moisture-retentive clay soils overlay freely-draining chalk at no great depth, ensuring that trees had adequate moisture during the summer but that excess winter rainfall drained away quickly—conditions which occur, for example, in west Hertfordshire. But he also had in mind places located at the foot of chalk escarpments, where rich loamy soils could be found, as in south Bedfordshire or south Cambridgeshire. Loamy, well-drained soils in general appealed to fruit growers. But we should not over-emphasise the importance of soils. Even where the local environmental conditions might appear unsuitable, large orchards, and concentrations of orchards, might nevertheless develop, if a local market—or good transport links to a distant one—existed. One additional factor is worth noting. Fruit growing was, for the most part, a small man's business. Where farms were too small to make a significant income from cereal growing or livestock rearing, especially in hard times, orchards often flourished. Fruit growing was closely associated with the cultivation of vegetables, in market-gardens. Orchards, and smallholdings, often went hand in hand.

Fruit growing was, by the middle decades of the twentieth century, a major industry in the eastern counties. Moreover, a number of important businesses in the region depended on the local fruit crop—and as we shall see, large amounts of cider were made here. Local growers had to take care to avoid planting in places where trees might be damaged by the frosts to which the east is susceptible, which could damage the blossom and thus the size of the final fruit crop. Overall, however, the warm and relatively dry summers which we enjoy in the region were good for the fruit harvest.

The wholesale disappearance of orchards from the landscape—their replacement by arable fields or housing, their conversion to gardens or pony paddocks—is a great loss, for a number of reasons. For centuries orchards were an indispensable part of everyday life, a central part of our culture, valued not only for the fruit they produced but also for their blossom, so cheerful a sight after the long winter months. Long-established orchards are also of great importance for biodiversity, with their combination of old, herb-rich grass and 'veteran' trees. Fruit trees age and become filled with the cavities and the rot required by a large number of rare organisms more quickly than other trees. Lichens, mosses, insects and fungi all flourish in old orchards (Figure 1.5). Some species are *only* found there, such as the Orchard Tooth Fungus, or the beetle known as the Noble Chafer— the latter no longer known in eastern counties. Orchards are important for many reasons, but the focus of this book is, as already explained, more limited. In the chapters that follow we will set out briefly the fruit-growing history of each of our eastern counties and discuss the various kinds of fruit grown in their orchards. And we present ways in which this can be used, providing recipes which we hope will be enjoyed by readers, and encourage them to seek out those places where 'traditional' varieties can still be acquired.

1.5 *Fruit trees age and 'veteranise' at a relatively early age, providing an important habitat for fungi, insects and much else.*

Hertfordshire
Down in the Cherry Orchards

HERTFORDSHIRE'S countryside is almost everywhere characterised by winding lanes, villages of timber-framed houses, scattered farms and old hedgerows. But there are subtle variations in this landscape from one part of the county to another. In the west, for example, we find the dramatic wooded hills of the Chilterns with their long, gentle dipslope extending to the south, cut by chalky valleys. In the east of the county, in contrast, the terrain is more gently rolling, with clay uplands which, while often well-wooded, have wider arable fields and fewer hedges. Yet much more dramatic and obvious are the variations in the degree of urbanisation within the county. By 1941 it could already be said that Watford and Barnet in the far south were 'largely dormitory areas for London', while other market towns in the south and west had 'entered a new phase: fast and efficient transport to London and to the Midlands combined with a local labour supply have attracted many light industries and much of south-west Hertfordshire has thus become greatly industrialised'. Over the following decades the establishment of 'New Towns' at Stevenage and Hatfield, and the expansion of the existing 'Garden Cities' at Letchworth and Welwyn, created a further band of urbanised land running north-south through the centre of the county, along the line of the A1. Today, pockets of countryside still exist in the west and south of Hertfordshire, some very attractive, but they give way abruptly to more built-up areas. It is in the east and the north-east of the county that the most extensive and continuous tracts of rural landscape survive.

At the start of the twentieth century there were well over 2,700 orchards in the county (Figure 2.1). Most were small and attached to farmhouses, providing fruit for the family and a small surplus for sale. Early documents suggest that such domestic orchards could be found almost everywhere, and that they were carefully managed. Trees were regularly replaced, and the grass beneath them was cut for hay and grazed with geese and sheep (leases for orchards, such as one for a farm in St Paul's Walden, dating to 1687, sometimes instructed the tenant not to keep cows there, presumably because they might damage the trees). Orchards were densely clustered in villages and market towns. When a property in Hoddesdon ('formerly "The Feathers" alehouse') was sold in 1882 it was described as being bounded by an orchard on its southern side and by

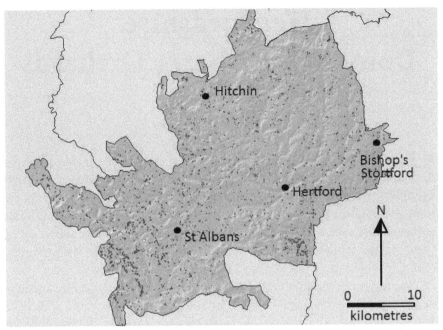

2.1. *The distribution of orchards in Hertfordshire in c. 1900. The dense concentration in the west includes the cherry orchards which were already a feature of the county by the start of the eighteenth century. County boundary as it was in the nineteenth century.*

another on its northern; it contained an orchard, and it included a small piece of land which was rented out as part of the orchard of Cherry Trees Farm! Some examples were short-lived features of the landscape but others survived for centuries. An orchard shown on a map of 1596 beside the farm called Clintons in Little Hadham was still in existence as late as the 1980s.

Some parts of the county were specialising in fruit production from an early date. In particular, orchards were particularly large and numerous in the area of countryside lying between St Albans, Berkhamsted, Rickmansworth and Watford. As early as 1797 the agriculturalist Arthur Young described how, in the 'south-west corner of the county … there are many orchards: apples and cherries are their principal produce'. One notable feature of this district, although one that was in decline by the time that Young was writing, was the practise of planting cherry and apple trees not only in orchards but also in the hedges around fields. The farmer and author William Ellis from Little Gaddesden recorded it as standard practice in the 1740s, and an undated map of a farm in Flaunden, drawn up around 1700, shows that most of the hedgerow trees were either cherries or apples (Figure 2.2). The loamy soils of the Chiltern dipslope were good for growing fruit, and London—less than 20 miles (30 kilometres) to the south-east—provided a ready market. Cherries were a particular speciality

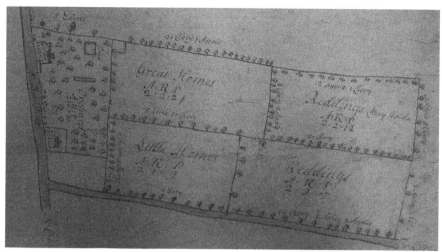

2.2 A map of a farm at Flaunden in west Hertfordshire, surveyed around 1700, showing the local custom of growing apples and cherries as hedgerow trees.

of this district. In 1864 James Clutterbuck described how the fruit was usually sold on the trees to dealers, realising between 12 shillings and 16 shillings per 'ped', or basket, holding 'about four dozen pounds'. The crop was profitable, but precarious. It was 'very often destroyed in a single night by an untimely frost'. He reported that some of the crop was used to make cherry brandy (see Cherry Bounce, below) and that the cherries were even used for dyeing.

The number of orchards in the west of the county increased steadily through the nineteenth century, as transport infrastructure improved, and by 1900 they were large and numerous here. Typical was an orchard at Croxley Green—one of many in the hamlet—which was run from 1893 until 1960 by the Stone family as part of a smallholding of 12 acres (5 hectares). When the orchard was first rented by Walter Stone the lease agreement described how he was to:

> Keep all trees properly pruned and when necessary substitute and plant young trees of good varieties. These should be properly planted, manured, staked and screened from damage by cattle or wind.

The orchard grew apples, pears but in particular cherries, the tall trees necessitating the use of very long ladders. The orchard is now a community open space, managed by Parish Council rangers and the Three Rivers District Council.

By 1900 there was also a noticeable concentration of orchards in the south-east of Hertfordshire, part of an important market-gardening area lying in and around the valley of the river Lea, again well positioned to serve London. Commercial orchards were also a feature of the far north of the county, in Ashwell and the villages around, where they formed an extension of the marked concentration which, as we shall see, existed in the south of the adjacent county of Cambridgeshire.

The expansion of suburbs in the first half of the twentieth century, in the south of Hertfordshire especially, led to the loss of some orchards. But new ones continued to be created. As a result of a series of acts of parliament, culminating in 1919, County Councils— including that for Hertfordshire—were empowered to purchase land to create smallholdings, latterly to provide employment for veterans returning from the First World War. Small orchards often formed part of these enterprises. A fine example of such a smallholding— complete with the original timber-clad smallholder's cottage with its cartshed/ piggery—survives in the Dunsley area on the eastern outskirts of Tring. It was originally tenanted by a Mr Jeacock and the orchard includes many of the trees planted soon after he took up the tenancy in 1920 (Figures 2.3 and 2.4).

2.3 (above) Jeacock's Farm, Tring, in Hertfordshire: a rare surviving example of an original County Council smallholder's cottage, erected in 1920.
2.4 (below) The orchard at Jeacock's Farm, lovingly maintained by the current tenant, Martin Hicks.

Through the first half of the twentieth century large numbers of commercial orchards were also planted by private individuals, encouraged both by the depressed state of conventional agriculture in the period before the outbreak of the Second World War and by the steady growth in the market for fruit, as local towns expanded and London grew inexorably. The fine example at Tewin, now managed as part of a wildlife reserve by the Hertfordshire and Middlesex Wildlife Trust, was established in 1931 by William Stenning Hopkyns. It covers around 4 hectares (c.10 acres) and was originally planted principally with Bramley cooking apples. Much of the produce of Hertfordshire orchards was taken to market by rail: being so close to London the railway network was remarkably dense, with few places in the county lying more than five miles from a station. When a commercial fruit-growing business was put up for sale at Great

Hormead in the north-east of the county in 1945 the particulars described how 'the vendor has been in the habit of sending his fruit to Spitalfields, the Boro' and Covent Garden Markets. During the last two seasons the Railway Company has collected the fruit from the orchards, put it on the rail and delivered to the markets.' The orchards, covering around 38 acres (15 hectares), contained 3,800 trees and had the previous year produced 9,000 bushels of apples and about 65 tons of plums. New commercial orchards—especially ones devoted to cherries—continued to be established in many parts of Hertfordshire into the 1960s but, as elsewhere, their numbers then went into sharp decline.

In Hertfordshire, as in other parts of England, large country houses also had their own orchards, often containing a very wide variety of fruit. In the sixteenth and seventeenth centuries, when large gardens were enclosed and highly 'formal' and geometric in their appearance, dwarf varieties of apple, pear, plum and cherry were liberally espaliered (trained) against the garden walls, accompanied by more exotic peaches and nectarines. But in addition, orchards often formed part of the ornamental grounds of the mansion, valued both for their fruit and for the beauty of their blossom. When, under the influence of 'Capability' Brown, walled gardens were cleared away from the vicinity of elite houses, so that mansions appeared to stand in open parkland, food producing areas were relegated to some more hidden location. But orchards remained important. They were usually placed beside the walled kitchen garden, within which fruit trees were also planted—still espaliered against the walls, or trained on metal arches over the paths, as can still be seen in the gardens at Woodcock Hill in Northchurch. Even in the early twentieth century orchards continued to be a major feature of the grounds of the large houses built in 'arts and crafts' style, like 'Amersfort' near Berkhamsted, designed by Ernest Willmott in 1911. Indeed, many of the larger suburban houses built in the county in the first half of the twentieth century were provided with extensive orchards.

A more striking feature of Hertfordshire's orchard heritage are what might be called 'institutional orchards'. Because the county lay so close to London, in the course of the nineteenth and twentieth centuries many large hospitals, mental asylums, children's homes and the like were built there, and these were often provided with large orchards to provide fruit for the kitchens and for everyday consumption. In many cases, the residents of such institutions worked in the orchards (as they did on the farms which were also attached to many examples). Hospital orchards also served a therapeutic role, providing a pleasant and calming place to walk under the spring blossom. Although many of these places no longer serve their original purpose, their orchards sometimes remain.

The Oval in Harpenden was originally established as a children's home in 1913 and its orchard—partly planted soon afterwards, and partly in the late 1940s—still contains more than fifty apple trees of more than twenty varieties. The example planted when Shenley mental hospital was opened in 1932 is now beautifully maintained by the Shenley Park Trust (the hospital was finally closed in 1998); the orchard which accompanied its sister institution, Harperbury, also survives, although in a sad and derelict condition and threatened with development. Just over the county's northern boundary in Bedfordshire, the Three Counties Asylum, serving Hertfordshire, Bedfordshire and Huntingdonshire, was opened in 1860 and was probably provided with an orchard, immediately to the west of the main buildings, from the start. Another, mainly planted with cooking apples, was added to the south east during or soon after the First World War. The hospital site has been redeveloped for housing but both orchards survive and are kept in excellent condition, one with a magnificent line of cobnuts—domesticated hazels—along its boundary. Perhaps the most striking of Hertfordshire's institutional orchards, however, is that attached to St Elizabeth's in Much Hadham, a centre for the care of epileptics which was established in 1903 and which still works with adults and children with complex needs. Planted in the inter-war years, it is one of three orchards originally associated with the home. It covers nearly 5 acres (c. 2 hectares) and contains around 140 trees, with 25 different varieties of apples alone, together with other fruit. It is lovingly maintained and rich in wildlife (Figure 2.5).

2.5 The magnificent orchard at St Elizabeth's Centre, Much Hadham in east Hertfordshire is one of the best surviving examples of an 'institutional' orchard in the county.

There do not appear to be any very ancient varieties of apples associated with Hertfordshire. William Ellis in 1744 singled out the Holland Pippin and the French Pippin as being amongst the most popular in the county but neither, as their names suggest, probably originated locally, while other varieties or types he notes, such as the 'Parsnip Apple', the Cat's Head or the Golden Rennet, were planted throughout the country. As in many other counties, the varieties most closely associated with Hertfordshire arose relatively late, and were in large measure developed, and disseminated, by commercial nurseries. Although there were many such businesses in the county from at least the eighteenth century, supplying fruit trees to both private individuals and commercial growers, the history of the Hertfordshire nursery industry is dominated by two companies— Lane's and Rivers'.

The latter was founded in Sawbridgeworth by John Rivers, who hailed from Basildon in Berkshire, as early as 1735 and during the nineteenth century, under the direction of Thomas Rivers (who took over the business in 1837), it became one of the foremost suppliers of fruit trees in England, as well as being noted for the development of techniques for fruit growing. In his book *The Orchard House; or the Cultivation of Fruit Trees in Pots* Thomas Rivers described how to grow diminutive fruit trees in pots in small glasshouses. These could be taken to the dining table for guests to pick their own dessert, or otherwise displayed! When the walled kitchen garden at Audley End, just over the county boundary in Essex, was restored a few years ago a replica orchard house, built to Rivers' original plan, was included as a feature.

Thomas Rivers developed numerous new varieties of fruit, by both selection and deliberate cross-breeding, and was most successful with his plums, especially Early Favourite and Early Prolific. He also introduced a number of new plum varieties from abroad, such as Précoce de Tours and Reine Claude Diaphane, further selecting and breeding from them and often changing their names. Additional plum varieties, including Rivers' Early Damson, were developed by his successors. Rivers also experimented successfully with new varieties of cherry and, in particular, of pear, travelling to France and Belgium to collect varieties (especially of the soft beurré pears) which he then propagated and marketed. He also seems to have pioneered what is now the standard practise of grafting pears onto root stocks of quince. His son, Thomas Frances Rivers, developed the Conference pear, a mid-season dessert variety which is now the most widely grown in England. It was so named because it was first exhibited at the Pear Conference held by the Royal Horticultural Society in 1888 at Chiswick, to discuss the threat faced by the industry from imported American and Canadian fruit.

The company was also responsible for a number of new apple varieties, including Rivers' Early Peach, Thomas Rivers, Rivers' St Martins, New Hawthornden and Rivers' Nonsuch, but only the first of these appears to have been widely cultivated. The nursery was, however, the first in England to market Cox's Orange Pippin, a variety first grown as a seedling by Richard Cox in Buckinghamshire; and it was the main producer of the popular cooking apple

2.6 The remains of Rivers' great nursery at Sawbridgeworth.

Warner's King, perhaps of Kentish origin, but acquired by the company from a nurseryman called James Warner of Garforth near Leeds. At its peak Rivers' was a large business. In the years around 1900 no less than 20,000 Early Prolific and Early Favourite bare-rooted plum trees were dispatched by the nursery each autumn. Trees were sent not only to private customers but also to other commercial nurseries, such as that of Wood and Ingram in Huntingdon. Following the death of Tom Rivers in 1978 the company was gradually wound down, finally closing in 1987. Parts of the nursery grounds survive, densely planted with fruit trees (Figure 2.6). The site has been studied, and is being actively preserved, by a dedicated group of volunteers, but faces an uncertain future.

Lane's of Berkhamsted was another important business. Established by Henry Lane some time around 1777 in St John's Well Lane, and continued by his son, also Henry, it expanded considerably under John Edward Lane in the second half of the nineteenth century and became one of the town's principal employers. The company ran both nurseries and commercial orchards. Some were located to either side of the town's High Street, others were in the outlying hamlets of Potten End and Bourne End. By 1902 Lane's reputedly had 20,000 apple, pear, plum and cherry trees growing on 60 acres (c. 24 hectares) of land, as well as 15 acres (6 hectares) devoted to cobnuts. Most of the fruit was, by this stage, being sent to Manchester and neighbouring industrial towns—the orchards were only a short distance from Berkhamsted station, on the direct line to the north-west. The nursery became well known for its grapevines, which were exported to France, Germany and other wine producing countries. But it was best known in England for an apple known as Lane's Prince Albert (Figure 2.7). This was discovered by Thomas Squire, a keen amateur gardener in the town, growing in the garden of a house called The Homestead. He propagated the tree and named it 'Victoria and Albert' following the visit of Queen Victoria and the

2.7 Lane's Prince Albert, probably the most famous of Hertfordshire's apple varieties.

Prince Consort to the town on 26th July 1841. The apple proved to be a good one and was marketed by Lane's—as 'Britain's Latest Apple'. Lane's declined in the inter-war years and closed shortly after the end of the Second World War.

Lane's Prince Albert is probably the most successful apple variety to have been developed in Hertfordshire. A good-sized cooker, juicy and rather acidic, it was widely planted and can still often be found in orchards today, in Hertfordshire and elsewhere. Rivers' Early Peach—first developed in 1893—and their 'Thomas Rivers'—first marketed a year earlier—were also quite successful apples at the time but are now rarely encountered. In contrast, Warner's King remains one of the more common apples found in old orchards while Cox's Orange Pippin, which Rivers' played a major role in popularising, is still quite widely planted, although to a lesser extent than at the peak of its popularity in the middle decades of the twentieth century.

Not all the varieties of apple associated with the county were developed by Lane's or Rivers'. Minor nurseries also made a contribution. The Brownlees Russet, for example—an intensely-flavoured, juicy and rather acidic dessert apple—was raised in 1848 by the Hemel Hempstead nurseryman William Brownlees. Others have obscure origins. The Hormead Pippin—a large yellow cooking apple—probably originated as a seedling in a garden or orchard in Great or Little Hormead in the north-east of the country around 1800, according to John Claudius Loudon, writing in 1835. But by this stage it was being cultivated in America, so its origins may be earlier. At the start of the twentieth century it was extensively propagated and marketed in England by the Kentish nursery company of Bunyard's, and old specimens can be found, thinly scattered, in orchards and gardens right across the country. The origins of the Hitchin Pippin—an eating apple with soft, pale yellow flesh, and a greenish-yellow skin with crimson stripes—are even more uncertain, but it was certainly in existence by 1896. It was never widely planted.

Several Hertfordshire varieties were developed by head gardeners on the estates of the gentry. The Aldenham Blenheim was discovered just after the First

2.8 *The Caroon cherry, as illustrated by George Bradshaw in his Pomona Britannica of 1812.*

World War by Edwin Beckett growing in the gardens at Aldenham House. It is a highly coloured version of the Blenheim Orange, a widely-planted variety which originated in the eighteenth century, but otherwise identical to it. More striking is the cooking apple known as the Bushey Grove, developed on the Bushey Hall or Bushey Grove estate, two and a half miles away, by J.T.Goode in 1897. It is a useful culinary variety, reducing quite quickly to a sharp but fruity purée, but is rarely found today and was probably never widely planted.

We should not, in a county like Hertfordshire, concentrate too much on apples. As noted, Rivers' developed a large number of plums and gages in their long history—at least 22 varieties, including Early and Blue Prolific—as well as a number of pears, most famously the Conference. But it is cherries with which Hertfordshire, perhaps more than any other English county except Kent, is most closely associated. Some of the varieties widely

2.9 Old Bramley's Seedling trees in Tewin orchard, now part of a nature reserve managed by the Hertfordshire and Middlesex Wildlife Trust.

grown in Hertfordshire were, once again, developed by Rivers'—most notably Early Rivers, first marketed in 1872. Archduke, which was sold by Rivers' almost since the nursery first opened, probably originated in Buckinghamshire but has a long association with the county. But many varieties of cherry—in contrast to apples—were long-established in Hertfordshire, of uncertain origin, and apparently local to the county's western cherry district. They include Bailey's Early Black, Strawberry Heart and the Caroon, also known as the Hertfordshire Black: all are especially associated with villages around Hemel Hempstead (Figure 2.8).

Some of the orchards mentioned above are open to the public and are well worth visiting, especially during blossom time or in the autumn, when the trees are laden with fruit. Stones Orchard at Croxley Green, which is managed as a public open space; Tewin Orchard, part of a wildlife reserve (Figure 2.9); Shenley orchard, part of a self-funded park; and the remains of Rivers nursery in Sawbridgeworth; are open all year round, free of charge. Others—Jeacock's in Tring, St Elizabeth's in Much Hadham, and that at the Three Counties Hospital, now known as 'Fairfields'—are only open on apple days and other special occasions. Also worth visiting are the many new community orchards which have been established in the county over the last few decades, many of which feature the classic Hertfordshire varieties we have discussed. There are fine examples at Aldbury, Baldock, Berkhamsted, Bushey,

Chorleywood, Codicote, Northaw, Oxhey and elsewhere. The town of St Albans may be unique in having four such orchards! All these wonderful places, maintained by volunteers, are doing much to keep Hertfordshire's rich orchard heritage alive.

Recipes

Baked Apple Dumplings (serves four)

William Ellis, who lived at Great Gaddesden in west Hertfordshire, described in his *Modern Husbandman* of 1744 how the large Catshead apple was 'a very useful apple to the farmer, because one of them pared and wrapped up in dough, serves with little trouble for making an apple-dumpling', for which purpose 'it has now got into such reputation in Hertfordshire ... that it is become the most common food with a piece of bacon or pickle-pork for families'. There are, in fact, several types of traditional dishes referred to as 'Apple Dumplings'. They vary in the type of pastry used, in whether the apples are used whole or sliced, and in how they are cooked. The pastry used can be suet, shortcrust or puff and the dumplings can be boiled, steamed or baked. There are many variations and related recipes, some with local names. Several can be found in the works of Hannah Glasse (writing in 1747) and Eliza Acton (writing in 1845).

2.10 Baked Apple Dumplings. Accounted a delicacy in Hertfordshire in the eighteenth century, and known throughout England. Lane's Prince Albert is ideal for this dish.

Lane's Prince Albert, which as described above originated in Berkhamsted in the mid nineteenth century, is ideal for this recipe but a Cox-type apple like Ribston Pippin or Orleans Reinette will do just as well. The Catshead apple so praised by Ellis is also suitable, if you can get hold of it! What is now the most popular English cooking apple, Bramley, is not suitable as it does not hold its shape when cooked.

Ingredients
Shortcrust Pastry made with 8 oz / 250 g plain flour, 2 oz / 130 g butter, 2 oz / 130 g lard (or vegetarian alternative), a pinch of salt, and a small amount of cold water to mix

4 medium sized apples, peeled and cored

A filling of your choice—choose from butter mashed with brown sugar and cinnamon, a mixture of dried fruit with sugar and lemon zest, mixed candied peel and lemon zest, mincemeat, quince jelly, or marmalade

Method
Make the pastry and leave to one side for at least 30 minutes (this prevents shrinkage during cooking).

Preheat the oven to 190°C / Gas Mark 5.

Peel, core and stuff the apples with your chosen filling.

Divide the pastry into four. Roll out each piece fairly thinly to form a circle large enough to wrap the apple in. Place each apple in the middle of its pastry circle. Dampen the edges of the pastry and draw it up around the apple. Pinch the pastry edges together to seal, and trim off any excess. Place on a greased baking sheet, with the join underneath. Use the pastry trimmings to make leaves to decorate the dumplings. Brush with beaten egg. Bake for 30 minutes until golden brown. Serve hot with custard or cream.

‽гр

Black Cherry Turnovers

William Hone described in 1857 how in certain parts of Hertfordshire—he presumably had the west of the county in mind—people had for centuries made cherry pasties 'which are by them highly esteemed for their delicious flavour'.

Entertainments called "the pasty feasts," in which the above mentioned "niceties" shine conspicuous, are always duly observed, and constitute a seasonal attraction "for all ages," but more particularly for the "juveniles", whose laughter-teeming visages, begrimed with the exuberant juice, present unmistakeable evidence of their "having a finger in the pie".

In her 1977 book *The Folklore of Hertfordshire*, Doris Jones-Baker suggested that the inhabitants of Frithsden in the Chilterns claimed to have invented 'the black cherry pasty and the cherry turnover', but whether or not this is true both were part of the traditional cuisine of Hertfordshire's cherry-growing district. Unfortunately, the recipes for both delicacies appear to have been lost. This recipe for 'Buckinghamshire Cherry Bumpers', included in the collections of both Mary Norwak and Sheila Hutchins, is probably close. Frithsden lies a short distance from the border with Buckinghamshire, and the west Hertfordshire cherry-growing district extended into that county.

Ingredients
450 g / 1 lb black cherries, preferably Bailey's Early Black if available

75 g / 3 oz caster sugar

250 g / 8 oz shortcrust pastry (see the Baked Apple Dumpling recipe above)

Method
Stone the cherries, place in a bowl and sprinkle with the sugar.

Preheat the oven to 200°C / 180°C Fan / Gas Mark 6.

2.11 Black Cherry Turnovers were widely eaten in west Hertfordshire in the past.

Roll out the pastry to a thickness of about 0.5 cm / ¼ inch. Use a pastry cutter to cut 10cm / 4 inch circles. Place a tightly-packed heap of cherries in the centre of each pastry circle. Dampen the edges of the pastry with water, fold it over to cover the cherries, and pinch the edges together to seal. Bake for 20—30 minutes, dredge with extra caster sugar, and eat hot or cold.

Another traditional speciality of west Hertfordshire is Cherry Bounce, a liqueur made from steeping cherries with sugar in brandy (in the manner of Sloe Gin): see the recipe for Damson Gin in Chapter 3. Cherry Bounce was not only made in west Hertfordshire but also in other cherry growing districts in the eastern counties. A recipe for Cherry Bounce, described as being 'from Littleport' in the Cambridgeshire Fens, appears in Joan Poulson's Old Anglian Recipes.

₧₧

Summer Fruit Salad

This recipe is based on the Archduke, a very old cherry variety, known to John Parkinson writing in 1629 and described by Forsyth in 1802. Although it possibly originated in Buckinghamshire, it was grown by Rivers, probably from the time the nursery opened, and was widely cultivated in the cherry orchards of west Hertfordshire. Ripening in June and July, it has red, tender, juicy sweet flesh. This is, however, a very flexible recipe: other kinds of dessert cherries can be substituted and you can use a mixture of whatever other soft fruit you have to hand. We have not included quantities in this recipe as it will depend on the number of different fruits used.

Ingredients
A mixture of soft fruit

Caster sugar or icing sugar to taste

Orange zest and juice, or a few drops rosewater or orange flower water (optional)

Method
Begin by taking a large decorative glass bowl. Wash and dry the cherries, remove the stalks and cut them in half, removing the stones. Place the halved cherries in the bowl. Do not wash raspberries (or tayberries or loganberries) as this will make them soggy. Add them to the bowl, mixing gently. Wipe strawberries gently with moistened kitchen paper, hull them, and depending on size, keep whole or cut into halves or quarters. Add them to the bowl and mix gently. Red and white currants should be

washed, shaken dry, and destalked before adding to the bowl. Nectarines can be added, washed, stoned and then cut into small chunks. Should you be lucky enough to have a mulberry tree, or to know someone who does, these can be added too. Black mulberries (often a dark purply red—mulberries are very confusing!) are the juiciest and have the most flavour. However, a note of caution here. Mulberries do not keep long or travel well. It is best to pick them just before use. A little sugar can be added to taste (this depends on the tartness of the fruit and personal taste). Some orange zest, along with a little freshly squeezed orange juice, can be added, or a few drops of rosewater or orange flower water. Cover and chill before serving with double cream or Greek yoghurt.

This mixture, minus the nectarine, can also be used as the base for a Summer Pudding.

2.12 Archduke Cherries, grown in west Hertfordshire for at least three centuries, make a perfect ingredient for a summer fruit salad.

∞∞

Apple Compôte

Warner's King is a culinary apple dating back to the 1700s which, as noted above, was strongly associated with Rivers' nursery in Sawbridgeworth. It was originally known as King Apple (in Forsyth's book of 1802, 'pomroy'). It cooks to a sharp, strongly flavoured purée and is therefore very suitable for recipes such as Apple Compôte, Apple Sauce and Apple Sauce Cake. Bramley apples can also be used and, if you prefer an uneven texture, apples which hold their shape when cooked (such as Lane's Prince Albert, or even dessert apples) can be added.

Ingredients
Apples, as above

Lemon zest and juice

Soft dark brown sugar

Method
Peel, core and roughly chop the apples, then place them in a heavy-based saucepan. Add lemon zest and juice, and the sugar. Stir to mix. Over a gentle heat, cook the apple until soft, stirring from time to time to make sure it doesn't burn. Add a few drops of water if necessary. Break up the soft apple with a wooden spoon. Add more sugar to taste, as needed. This is a very flexible recipe. It is really good with Greek yoghurt—either as a pudding or for breakfast. It can be carefully folded into lightly whipped cream or custard to make a fool, which in turn could also be frozen to make an ice cream.

Using white sugar, and in smaller quantities, it makes good apple sauce to serve with roast pork or goose.

Unsweetened apple purée can be used to make Apple Sauce Cake.

ೞೞ

Pear, Blue Cheese and Walnut Salad (starter, serves six)

This is a modern recipe designed around the Conference pear which, as described above, was developed in the late nineteenth century by Thomas Francis Rivers at Sawbridgeworth. Conference is now one of the most widely available pears, but other kinds of dessert pear can also be used.

Ingredients
1 ½ Conference pears

150 g blue cheese (Stilton, Shropshire Blue, Roquefort etc but not Danish Blue which is rather too harsh for this recipe)

75 g walnut pieces

1 bag rocket leaves

1 tsp wholegrain mustard

Sea salt

Freshly milled black pepper

1 clove garlic, crushed

1 tbsp grapeseed or groundnut oil

1 tbsp walnut oil

2 teaspoons perry vinegar, if available (if not, use cider vinegar)

Method
First make the dressing. Mix the mustard, salt, pepper, garlic, oils and vinegar. Whisk together or shake in a screwtop jar.

Core but do not peel the pears. Quarter them and then cut each quarter lengthways into 3 slices. In a bowl, toss the pear slices in the dressing (to prevent them from going brown).

Toast the walnuts by dry-frying them. Watch them—once they start to brown they do so very quickly and can easily burn. Tip them immediately on to a non-metallic plate and leave them to cool.

Crumble the cheese or cut into small cubes.

To assemble the salad, first arrange a handful of rocket leaves on each individual plate. Then place 3 pear slices on top of the leaves and scatter the cheese and walnuts over the top. Lastly, drizzle the rest of the dressing over the leaves and around the plate.

Serve with walnut bread.

Bedfordshire
Wardens, Prunes and Clangers

B EDFORDSHIRE is a very different county to Hertfordshire. Lying further from London it was not—until very recent decades—seriously affected by suburbanisation, except in the immediate vicinity of rail stations on main lines, as around Ampthill. It has, of course, long had some large towns—especially Bedford in the centre and Luton in the south. On the clays to the south of Bedford, a major brick industry developed through the twentieth century. But this has now largely disappeared again, and in general the county remains, in spite of recent rapid development, less built up than Hertfordshire. Yet if the county is more rural, its countryside is in general less picturesque, more workaday. To the south it extends into the Chilterns but its other main range of hills—the Greensand Ridge—is uninspiring, if attractive. Running diagonally across the county, it separates extensive tracts of lower-lying, more gently rolling clayland. Unlike most of Hertfordshire, moreover, Bedfordshire is a land of villages, rather than scattered farms and small hamlets, although there are exceptions to this (especially in the north of the county) and the villages themselves are often large, sprawling and irregular, with numerous named 'Ends'—almost like a collection of hamlets that happened to come together. And in contrast to Hertfordshire, where most of the fields have ancient origins, much of Bedfordshire lay in 'open fields'—vast areas without hedges where the lands of individual proprietors lay intermixed—until these were enclosed in the eighteenth or nineteenth century. For the most part, the straight hawthorn hedges which border Bedfordshire's fields are a relatively recent creation.

Bedfordshire was never really noted for its orchards. In part this may have been because the existence of extensive open fields, hemming in villages on all sides, made it difficult to establish them on any scale; in part because of the predominance of heavy clay soils, unsuitable for fruit growing; and in part because it lay remote from London. In 1808 the agriculturalist Thomas Batchellor described how

> The orchards are in general very small in this county. There are a few that may contain a 100 fruit trees of various kinds, and new ones of an acre or two may be occasionally met with, planted sometimes in squares of about

seven yards between each tree, but there are frequently no other orchards than what are included in the gardens, consisting of four or five trees.

Cherries were grown in the south of the county, as Batchellor also noted, forming a continuation of the cherry-growing district of the west Hertfordshire Chilterns. But most of the small orchards found in Bedfordshire were filled with apple trees, accompanied by smaller numbers of pears and plums.

In the course of the nineteenth century, in Bedfordshire as elsewhere, there seems to have been a general increase in the number of orchards, and in their extent. By 1900, to judge from the Ordnance Survey maps, there were a little over 2,000 in the county—although given Bedfordshire's size this was a density significantly less than in Hertfordshire or, indeed, any of the other counties in

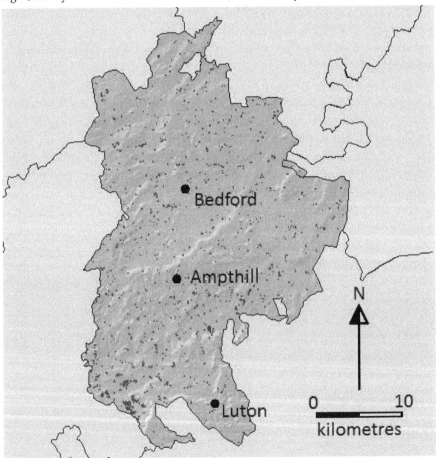

3.1 *The distribution of orchards in Bedfordshire in c. 1900. The concentration in the far south-west of the county represents the Aylesbury 'Prune' district. County boundary as it was in the nineteenth century.*

eastern England. Orchards were, for the most part, evenly spread across the county. But there were clusters around Bedford itself, and a particularly large concentration in the south, on the light loamy soils at the foot of the Chiltern escarpment (Figure 3.1). Many of these southern orchards, especially towards the west—in an area extending into the Vale of Aylesbury in Buckinghamshire— were largely or exclusively devoted to the cultivation of 'Aylesbury Prunes'.

The 'prune' was not a 'prune' in the usual sense of the word—that is, it was not a dried plum, but a small dark cooking plum or late eater, a cultivar of the damson (Figure 3.2). It may have been grown in local orchards for decades but production escalated from the 1840s. By the end of the century orchards specialising in 'Aylesbury Prunes' were large and numerous in a band, two or three miles wide, extending for some twelve miles from Weston Turville in Buckinghamshire in the south-west to Stanbridge and Totternhoe in the north-east. By 1900 vast areas of orchards existed in villages like Totternhoe, Billington, Eggington and Slapton: there were well over a hundred separate orchards in Eaton Bray alone, extending collectively over 50 hectares (Figure 3.3). There are even references to the cultivation of Aylesbury Prunes, apparently on a commercial basis, in the churchyard here. Most of the

3.2 The famous Aylesbury Prunes, a variety of damson grown in the orchards of south-west Bedfordshire and the adjacent parts of Buckinghamshire.

fruit was taken, packed in baskets or 'skips', to London, via the railway station at Cheddington, just over the county boundary in Buckinghamshire, or the halt at Stanbridge. But some went north to Bolton, Manchester, Wigan or Liverpool. Indeed, the development of the industry seems to have followed hard on the heels of the arrival of the railways—Cheddington station opened in 1838—and also the enclosure of the open fields, which came very late to many of the parishes in the district. Eaton Bray for example was mainly enclosed by parliamentary act in 1861, Totternhoe as late as 1891 (it was the last village in Bedfordshire to be enclosed).

Many of the Prune orchards were also used by local farmers for fattening

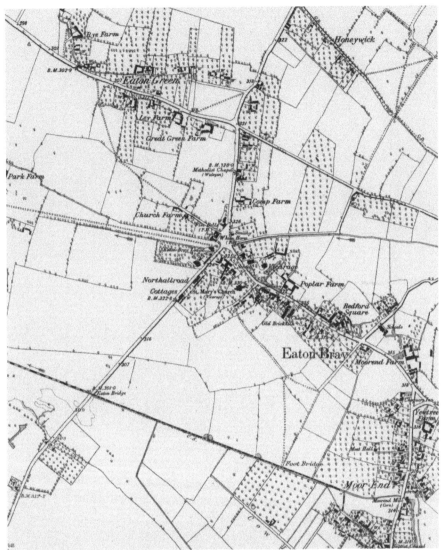

3.3 *Extract from the 6-inch Ordnance Survey map of 1880 showing the density of orchards in Eaton Bray, in the heart of the Bedfordshire 'Prune' country.*

Aylesbury Ducks. There is, moreover, a persistent tradition that the damsons were used for dyeing military uniforms and in the hat trade in Luton, although there is no hard evidence to support it. The south Bedfordshire orchards did not, however, only specialise in 'Prunes'. Many also grew apples, cherries and, in particular, other kinds of damson. When the northern portion of the Ashridge estate was placed on the market in 1911, including much land straddling the Buckinghamshire and Bedfordshire border in 'prune country', several of the farms were described as having 'enclosures of Orchard Land planted with Prune and Damson trees in full bearing'.

During the first half of the twentieth century the southern orchards continued to flourish. Their numbers increased—by the 1950s they covered almost a square kilometre of land in Eaton Bray alone. But orchards also expanded in other parts of the county, especially in villages on the Greensand Ridge such as Clophill, Maulden and Husbourne Crawley, some associated (as in Hertfordshire) with County Council smallholdings. One development of note was the establishment of an orchard and small fruit business by the Hartley's jam company at Holwell Bury in Shillington, on the county boundary with Hertfordshire. The estate was placed on the market in 1898 and, as *The Victoria County History* described in 1908, 'that portion which includes the old farm-house and buildings has been purchased by Mr Hartley of Liverpool, and is now used as a fruit-growing farm'. William Pickles Hartley ran what became the largest wholesale grocers in Lancashire and began to produce jam in 1871, eventually coming to concentrate almost entirely on this side of his business. His jam factory moved from Bootle to Liverpool in 1886, and by 1912 Hartley's were the largest jam makers in the world. The Holwell Bury farm was conveniently located a little over a kilometre to the south of Henlow Station on the main line to St Pancras in London (in 1901 Hartley's had opened a factory in Bermondsey, to cater for the London market) and although mainly devoted to soft fruit like strawberries it included nearly 40 hectares of orchards, mainly growing plums.

Perhaps the most interesting commercial venture of the inter-war years, however, was the Cox's Orange Pippin Orchard company. In 1929 part of the Cockayne Hatley estate, on the claylands of north-east Bedfordshire, was acquired by John Alexander Whitehead for a 'very reasonable sum'. Whitehead had previously been involved in a number of business ventures in both Britain and the USA and appears to have bought the estate with the intention of planting apple orchards. He aimed at intensive production, using a clone of Cox's Orange Pippin which had recently been developed at the Long Ashton Research Station near Bristol, grafted onto rootstock which produced trees of compact growth and not exceeding 8 feet in height. Worcester Pearmains and James Grieve were planted as pollinators. By 1931 2,000 trees had been planted; two years later the number had risen to 30,000 (Figure 3.4). At this point,

3.4 *Workers in the orchards of the Cox's Orange Pippin Orchards company near Cockayne Hatley in the 1930s.*

however, Whitehead decided on a policy of more rapid expansion, funded by a range of private investors, and set up his Cox's Orange Pippin Orchard company (COPO). He targeted small investors, who were described as 'treeholders' in his first publicity leaflet. For £30 a subscriber could become the proud owner of 90 Cox's and 15 Worcester Pearmains. He or she would receive the profits from the fruit eventually produced, minus cultivation and other costs. More than 2,000 individuals—many of them women—signed up, attracted by Whitehead's claims that they would, in addition to making money, be providing rural employment and increasing the country's self-sufficiency in food. But in 1934 the business model was changed. While trees could still be bought in sets, individuals could also now buy a single tree for 10 shillings and then recruit further members—receiving 4 shillings for every one recruited above an initial two—in what we would today describe as a pyramid selling scheme. By 1936, 5,000 people had subscribed and £500,000 had been raised. Whitehead purchased most of the remainder of the Cockayne Hatley estate as well as other land in the county (and also Stonebury Hall Farm in Buntingford in Hertfordshire). He built a large packing shed, workshops and other facilities, and invited existing investors to an annual 'Apple Blossom Day', where they could enjoy viewing their investment. Visits were encouraged more generally: 'membership entitles the member to visit the orchards, nurseries and gardens at any time, to picnic in the grounds, to be provided with hot water for tea, play tennis, go boating on the lake and to generally make one's self at home.'

By 1939 over 2.5 million trees had been planted and more than 200 people were employed in the orchards. But the heavy clay at Cockayne Hatley was not well suited to fruit trees, the claims made by Whitehead regarding the future value of the investments were overstated, and he siphoned off some of the money into other business ventures. The orchards were profitable in 1936, just profitable in 1937, and then made increasing losses. The 'treeholders' were held to be financially liable for these, and subscriptions dried up. Whitehead proposed a number of legally dubious forms of further investment, and in 1940 wrote to each of the 'treeholders' claiming that the local War Agricultural Committee was demanding that large areas of the orchards should be planted with potatoes, and that the costs of 'certain works of cultivation' needed to be met by them at an estimated rate of £1 5sh per 100 trees. Unfortunately for Whitehead, his accountant informed the Biggleswade police that all this was untrue, and he was prosecuted. Although the case against him was finally dismissed in the Old Bailey, the judge ruled that this particular part of the scheme should end, and that Whitehead should return £1,000 he had taken out of the business. In the event, parts of the orchards were turned over to arable crops during the war. More importantly Whitehead, short of capital, was obliged to mortgage parts of the estate, and following a particularly

3.5 Inspecting the new apple store at Bromham House in 1903.

bad harvest in 1946 the property was sold to the Co-operative Wholesale Society. They continued to run the orchards until 1974, when they were grubbed up. Little remains today except the huge packing shed.

In Bedfordshire, as in Hertfordshire, large orchards could be found attached to large institutions, although—more distant from London, and more thinly populated—there were fewer of these in the county: the Three Counties Asylum in the far south east, close to the county boundary, has already been discussed. And in Bedfordshire, as elsewhere, great country houses had their orchards, and invested heavily in the facilities for both growing and storing fruit (Figure 3.5). Before the mid eighteenth century such orchards often formed part of the ornamental grounds, as at Wrest Park near Silsoe; later they were relegated to a more sequestered location, beside the kitchen garden (in 1791 the Duke of Bedford bought eighty dwarf apple trees and 80 dwarf pear trees from Samuel Swinton's nursery in Sloane Street, London for his new kitchen garden at Woburn Abbey). And as in Hertfordshire, large suburban houses might, in the late nineteenth and early twentieth centuries, be similarly provided with extensive orchards, although as noted suburban expansion was more muted in Bedfordshire. Typical was a house in The Avenue, Ampthill, advertised for sale in 1910:

A most desirable and substantially built freehold residence known as High Knoll, built by the late Mr G Shaw for his own occupation in 1903. With stable, coach house and greenhouse, together with the ornamental pleasure and kitchen gardens which are most productive and contain upwards of 40 varieties of apple, pear, plum and other fruit trees … the whole embracing an area of about 1 acre, 16 poles and commanding, extensive and unobstructed views towards the south.

A number of old fruit varieties have been associated with Bedfordshire, although not always reliably. One is the Aylesbury Prune, although this more probably originated over the county boundary in Buckinghamshire, or possibly even further west, in Berkshire. Another is the Bedfordshire Greening apple, although this has disappeared without trace, last recorded in the late nineteenth century. The Bedfordshire Foundling, still occasionally seen in old gardens, is also an old apple, first recorded around 1800, which presumably originated in the county. The most important, although contentious, candidate for 'ancient Bedfordshire variety' is, however, the Warden Pear (Figure 3.6).

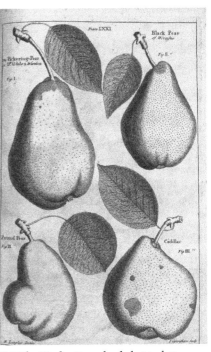

3.6 The Warden Pear, closely but perhaps erroneously associated with Old Warden in Bedfordshire. An illustration from Batty Langley's Pomona or the Fruit Garden Illustrated of 1729.

By the fifteenth century the term 'warden' was being used to describe a wide range of cooking pears, used in a variety of dishes, including the Warden Pies referred to in Shakespeare's *Winter's Tale* ('I must have Saffron to colour the Warden Pies') and 'Wardouns in Sirop' described below. Wardens were also used to make a sweetmeat with medicinal properties known as *Chardewarden* (literally 'flesh of warden'). The term was often employed for the larger culinary pears but some wardens appear to have been quite small, and what such pears really had in common is the fact that they never truly ripened and needed to be cooked to be edible, and that they were good keepers, remaining edible, if stored in the right conditions, until the spring.

The connection with Bedfordshire is that the Cistercian Abbey of Old Warden included, from the fifteenth century, three pears in its coat of arms, giving rise to a widespread belief that wardens were first developed by the monks there. But wardens are recorded from all over the country in the previous centuries and feature prominently, for example, in an early fifteenth-century manuscript written at Spalding Priory in Lincolnshire. On balance, it seems more likely that Old Warden Abbey adopted the fruit as a 'logo' because of its name. 'Warden' as a term for a type of pear more probably came from the Anglo-Norman word warder, meaning 'to preserve or maintain', alluding to the keeping qualities of the fruit, whereas the Abbey took its name from the village in which it stood, which in turn probably derived its name from the Old English 'weard', meaning 'watch', and 'dun' meaning 'hill', the place being located at one of the highest points along the Greensand Ridge. All this said, the abbey arms do suggest that the community felt a particular affinity with the fruit, and almost certainly cultivated it in their grounds. The association of warden pears with Old Warden is so widely accepted that it would be churlish not to offer it at least an honorary status as a Bedfordshire fruit.

Overall, however, there are few ancient varieties associated with the county, not surprisingly perhaps given that, before the mid nineteenth century, Bedfordshire was not really noted for its orchards. In the nineteenth century, a number of new varieties were nurtured by the head gardeners on some of the county's large landed estates: the apple varieties Desse de Buff, Earl Cowper, and probably Queenby's Glory all originated in the gardens of Wrest Park near Silsoe in the nineteenth century. But, even more than in Hertfordshire, the fruit varieties most closely associated with the county were mainly developed by commercial nurseries, and by one nursery business above all others—Laxton's.

The firm was founded by Thomas Laxton, who was born in Tinwell in the county of Rutland and who became a solicitor before developing an interest in botany and, in particular, plant hybridisation, corresponding for a time with Charles Darwin. By 1879 he had moved to Bedford and set up business as a 'seed grower and merchant' in Harpur Street, where he concentrated on developing new varieties of strawberry. But under his two sons, Edward Augustine Lowe Laxton and William Hudson Lowe Laxton, the family came to be associated with the development of new breeds of apples, pears and plums. The brothers went into business together—as 'Laxton Brothers'—in Bedford in 1888. Using the breeding methods developed by their father they were responsible for producing no less than 22 new varieties of apple, eight of pear and eighteen of plum (as well as further new types of strawberry). Originally based in Bromham Road in Bedford, they subsequently opened a shop at 63a High Street and by 1900 operated the 140-acre (57-hectare) Tollgate Nursery in Goldington Road.

3.7 'Superb', first marketed in 1897, is one of the most successful of the apple varieties developed by Laxton's of Bedford.

Some of the most successful fruit varieties in history, many still widely found in gardens today, were produced by the company, mainly between 1895 and 1925. The apples were mostly dessert varieties, such as Laxton's Superb (1897) (Figure 3.7), Laxton's Epicure, Laxton's Fortune (1904); Lord Lambourne (1907); and Laxton's Favourite (1925). All were developed by cross-pollinating established varieties. Laxton's Fortune, for example—a sweet apple with a pale yellow skin, mottled with flecks of red—was a cross between Cox's Orange Pippin and Wealthy; Lord Lambourne, a rather aromatic apple with greenish flesh and a golden skin, flushed maroon, was the result of crossing James Grieve with Worcester Pearmain. The most successful of Laxton's plum varieties were perhaps Early Laxton, first marketed in 1916, a medium-sized yellow-skinned dessert plum with juicy, slightly pinkish flesh (a cross of Catalonia and Early Rivers, described above, pp.17); and Laxton's Cropper, a cross of the Victoria plum and the Aylesbury Prune—a fairly large, blue-black cooking plum, first marketed in 1906. After several decades of success, the business came to an end in 1957, when it went into voluntary liquidation and the shop and nursery were sold.

The success of Laxton's, and the extent to which fruit varieties developed by them can be found in orchards and gardens throughout the country, arguably represents Bedfordshire's greatest contribution to the nation's orchard heritage. Wonderful collections of the apples, pears and plums developed by the company can be seen at the Park Wood local nature reserve and community orchard, Hill Drive, Bedford and at Mowsbury Hillfort, Ravensden, on the outskirts of Bedford. Both are open to the public. Other orchards in the county which are well worth visiting include Southill Community Orchard, Southill, near Biggleswade; Great Billington Community Orchard, Great Billington, near Leighton Buzzard; and Corn Close Community Orchard at Riseley. There are, unfortunately, no long-established orchards which can be visited in Bedfordshire. But a trip to the south, to look at the few surviving damson orchards—now degraded and largely derelict—is strongly recommended. The best survivals are around Eaton Green in Eaton Bray, where the old damson trees can be viewed from the public footpath, growing on the ridge-and-furrow earthworks marking the strips of the earlier village open fields, the whole making for a wonderful, layered piece of landscape history (Figure 3.8).

3.8 One of the surviving 'Prune' orchards at Eaton Bray in Bedfordshire.

Recipes

Bedfordshire Clanger (makes 4-6)

Perhaps the most famous fruit dish associated with the county is the Bedfordshire Clanger, although versions can also be found in neighbouring counties. Indeed, it is sometimes described as a Hertfordshire Clanger, and in the west of that county was also known as a Trowley Dumpling. Today it is usually suggested that clangers were elongated pasties containing meat at one end and apple at the other, but traditionally these were called "'alf an 'alf", with the true clanger being savoury only. Recorded fillings include liver and onion, bacon and potatoes, and pork and onion: sage was often used as a flavouring. Nineteenth-century writers suggest that clangers were made by the wives of agricultural labourers, and taken into the field as a mid-day meal. The filling was enclosed in suet pastry and either

3.9 *The famous Bedfordshire Clanger. This is, strictly speaking, an "'alf an 'alf".*

baked or boiled in a cloth. There is some discussion about whether the pastry was to be eaten or was just there to protect the filling. The baked Bedfordshire Clanger was revived in the 1990s by Gunns, a local baker in Sandy, Biggleswade and Bedford. They have devised a range of fillings, including such innovations as Lamb Mint and Veg with Plum Jam and Bombay Veg Curry with Mango! A recipe for Onion Clanger appears in Pippa Gomar's 1988 Cambridgeshire Country Recipes and for some time featured on the menu in the tearoom of the National Trust's Peckover House in Wisbech. This is a more traditional version, although it does include a sweet filling as well as the savoury so it is, technically, an "'alf an 'alf".

Ingredients
Suet Pastry:
500 g / 1 lb plain white flour

225 g / 8 oz beef suet

12 tbsps water

Savoury Filling:
450 g / 1 lb minced pork

½ onion, chopped

Sage leaves, chopped

1 small potato diced

Salt

Freshly milled pepper

Sweet Filling:
1 medium apple, peeled, cored and chopped small. A Cox-type dessert apple works best.

Beaten egg, to glaze

Method
Make the pastry and leave it to rest for 30 minutes.

Preheat the oven to 210° / gas 6 ½.

Prepare the fillings. Mix the savoury ingredients. Prepare the apples (toss in a little lemon juice to stop them turning brown).

Divide the pastry into 4 or 6 (they are very filling!). Roll the pastry into rectangles twice the size of the finished clanger (which resembles a large sealed sausage roll). Place a pastry strip on top of the pastry to divide the 2 fillings. Place the savoury filling on half the pastry at one end, and the sweet on the same half of the pastry at the other (you will need to fold the other half over the filling). Brush all round the edge with water and fold the rest of the pastry over the filling. Seal the edges. Mark the sweet end by scoring the pastry. Brush with beaten egg.

Bake for 30 minutes. They are best eaten hot but can also be eaten cold.

സര

Sautéed Apple with Bacon, New Potatoes and Shallots

Unlike the previous recipe, this is a modern dish which makes a good light lunch or supper. It is designed around one of Laxton's most successful varieties—Lord Lambourne—usually considered a dessert apple, but excellent when cooked and ideal for this recipe as it holds its shape well. If this is unavailable choose a Cox-like variety, or a Reinette such as Ashmead's Kernel which, as well as keeping its shape, has a good balancing acidity and crisp texture. It would also be good to choose a variety with a colourful skin.

Ingredients
Shallots, peeled and roughly chopped

Unpeeled waxy new potatoes, boiled until just tender and cut into chunks or, if very small, left whole

Smoked streaky bacon, cut into pieces

Dessert apples (preferably Lord Lambourne --- see note above), unpeeled, cored and cut into chunks

Olive or Bedfordshire rapeseed oil

Salt

Freshly milled black pepper

A few sage leaves, roughly chopped

A few juniper berries, crushed using a pestle and mortar

Note: we have left quantities up to you as proportions will depend on personal taste and availability.

As a rough guide, use roughly equal quantities of apple and potatoes with a tablespoon of oil, a medium shallot, and 2 rashers of bacon per person.

Method
Heat the oil in a frying pan or sauté pan. Fry the shallots over medium heat until they are beginning to soften.

Add the bacon and cook until it becomes opaque.

Add the potato, apple, crushed juniper berries, sage and seasoning (not too much salt as the bacon will be salty—you can always add more if necessary before serving). Continue to cook over medium to high heat, stirring until browned.

Adjust seasoning as necessary and serve.

(Variation: try adding cubes of winter squash to the softening shallots and cook until they become tender, stirring frequently to prevent burning, before adding the bacon).

ಬಃಆ

Wardouns in Sirop, or Pears in Red Wine

As we noted earlier, 'warden' pears did not originate in Old Warden in Bedfordshire. Indeed, the warden was not one specific variety but was a generic name for number of hard cooking pears. Nevertheless, the popularity and antiquity of the association with Bedfordshire are such that it would be unreasonable not to include a recipe using wardens in this section of the book. Pears in Red Wine is a dish we are familiar with today, but this is a modern version of its medieval ancestor. If warden-type pears are not available, use underripe dessert pears, but be aware that this will considerably reduce the cooking time.

Ingredients

Hard pears, 1 per person (unless using the rather large varieties Catillac or Uvedale St Germain, when 1 pear will serve 2). Choose pears for their shape as you want them to sit upright when serving

Red wine, enough to come at least halfway up the pears when laid on their sides. Approx 1 pint / 600 ml for 8 pears. We recommend using Shiraz for its spicy flavour and rich, purply colour. Medieval recipes cook the pears with mulberries for their colour

Caster sugar, approx. 2 oz / 50 g, but this will depend on your choice of wine and personal preference

2 whole cinnamon sticks (Do not be tempted to use ground cinnamon, as the liquid will look cloudy and have an unpleasant grainy texture)

Bay leaves, 1 per pear

Edible gilding (available from sugarcraft suppliers and some supermarkets), optional

Method

Preheat the oven to 130°C / Fan 110°C / Gas ½. Peel the pears carefully, keeping the stalk intact. You can leave the pears whole or core them very carefully from underneath (note: cored pears will take less time to cook). Cut a very thin slice off the bottom of the pear so it will sit upright.

Choose a wide flameproof casserole, large enough to take the pears lying on their sides in a single layer, with a tight-fitting lid. Place the prepared pears on their sides in the casserole. Pour over the red wine, sprinkle with the sugar and add the cinnamon sticks at either end of the casserole.

On the hob, bring the contents of the casserole very gently to simmering point. Cover the casserole and place in the oven.

Cook until they are tender (test with the point of a sharp knife) but not too soft. Large wardens may take 3 hours or more (1 ½ hours per side). Small underripe dessert pears may take 1 ½ hours (45 minutes per side) or less. Halfway through cooking time, turn the pears over very gently.

When cooked, discard the cinnamon sticks and transfer the pears (still on their sides) and the cooking liquid to a container, cover and chill. It is best to cook the pears a couple of days in advance. They will continue absorbing the spiced wine. Turn the pears in the wine every few hours so they absorb the colour from the wine evenly.

Gild fresh bay leaves with edible gilding, or alternatively leave them ungilded.

To serve, place the pears sitting upright in a shallow dish, large enough for them to sit comfortably surrounded by the wine. Pour the cooking liquid over the pears. Using a sharp knife, make a small slit next to the stalk. Gently slot a bay leaf in each slit.

(Variations: try using a good quality dry cider instead of red wine; or use different whole spices, such as star anise or cloves).

3.10 Pears in Red Wine—a modern take on the medieval recipe ' Wardouns in Sirop'.

❧☙

Damson Fool

The damsons known as Aylesbury Prunes, historically the most important fruit produced in Bedfordshire, are like the rather similar 'Shropshire Prunes' now rather difficult to get hold of. Other damson varieties such as Merryweather or Farleigh will do just as well, but be aware that these are sweeter varieties (they are both more of a cross between a true damson and a domestic plum), so will require less sugar.

Ingredients

1 ½ lbs / 375 g damson—the quantity allows for the extra weight of the stones

A very small amount of water

6 oz / 190 g caster sugar, or to taste

½ pint / 10 fl oz / 300 ml double cream

3.11 Damson Fool—accompanied by a glass of Damson Gin (made with a mixture of Aylesbury Prune and Shropshire Prune).

Method

Halve the damsons and cook gently with a very little water (around 3 tbsps) until soft. This next bit is hard work but definitely worth it! Rub the cooked damsons through a nylon sieve to remove the stones and skin. You don't want to lose any of the precious damson flesh. Add sugar to taste to the damson purée and leave until cold.

Whip the cream to the soft peak stage, taking care not to overwhip it. Gradually fold in the puréed damsons. Chill before serving. This is the most glorious colour!

(This can be frozen to make a delicious ice cream.)

(Variations: try using different fruits. The normal proportions are 1 lb / 450 g fruit to ½ pint / 300 ml cream, with sugar to taste).

୫୦୧୫

Damson Gin

Sloe gin was much consumed in Bedfordshire in the past, partly as a remedy for indigestion. This excellent recipe instead uses the damsons so closely associated with the county. It has an intense flavour.

Ingredients
Damsons.

Gin—1 pint / 600 ml for every 1 lb /450 g of damsons.

Sugar—the amount depends on how sweet you want it to be, and on the tartness of the damsons (see note above on varieties). As a rough guide, use 6 oz / 190 g for a dry liqueur, 12 oz / 375 g or even more for a sweet one.

Method

Prick the damsons in several places, and place in a kilner jar or similar, layered with the sugar. Pour the gin over the fruit and seal. Keep in a cool dark place and shake gently every day for a couple of weeks until the sugar has dissolved. Keep for 3 months and then strain and bottle it. Serve as an aperitif or after a meal.

(Variation: try using different fruit (as in Hertfordshire's Cherry Bounce) and prepare according to type—that is, slice larger fruit, use raspberries etc whole. Or try using different spirits, such as vodka, brandy or whisky!).

୫୦୯୨

Potton Apple Florentine

A florentine was a type of pastry which appears to have originated in France. It was introduced into England before 1570 and then continued to be popular into the late Georgian period. Although Florentines were made all over the country, the best existing description comes from Potton in Bedfordshire around 1770, as discussed by food historians Peter Brears and Elizabeth Ayrton. Peter Brears in *Cooking and Dining in Tudor and Early Stuart England* tells us that it 'consisted of an immensely large dish of pewter, or such-like metal, filled with good baking apples sugar and lemon to the brim; with a roll of rich paste as a covering—pie-fashion. When baked, before serving up, the upper crust .... was taken off and divided into sizeable triangular portions, which were again arranged around the dish in order, by way of garnish, and ...... a full quart of well-spiced ale was poured in, hissing hot.'

The dish is well worth making, but do NOT use a pewter receptacle (because of the lead content). Try using Peasgood's Nonsuch apples, technically not a Bedfordshire variety but one said to have been introduced by Thomas Laxton when living at Stamford, before his move to Bedford. Alternatively try Lord Lambourne. Bramleys will not be suitable for this dish. Bake at 200°C / Fan 180°C / Gas Mark 6 for approximately 35 minutes, or until the crust is a golden brown.

Essex
D'Arcy Spice and Tiptree Jam

ESSEX has a landscape which is similar in many respects to that of Hertfordshire. It has an old-enclosed countryside, albeit much damaged by modern farming, with winding lanes, species-rich hedges, scattered farms and small hamlets. And, lying close to London, it has like Hertfordshire been much affected by urban expansion and suburbanisation, especially in the south-east, and in a broad band flanking the A12, running through the centre of the county, from Brentford to Chelmsford and Colchester. More recently, development pressures have been intense all along the margins of the Thames estuary. Over much of the county the soils are not particularly conducive to commercial fruit-growing. Most of the north-west comprises heavy, damp boulder clay, while much of the south-east is characterised by cold, impervious London Clay. But light, well-drained loams also occur in a number of places, especially beside the Thames estuary and in the area around Colchester, while the market for fruit provided by London encouraged, over the last few centuries, the planting of orchards even on the less inviting soils.

Essex was for long a land of prosperous farms, and farm orchards loom large in documents from the sixteenth, seventeenth and eighteenth centuries. In 1597 John Battell of Eastwood left to his wife 'during her widowhood, yearly out of my orchard six bushels of the best apples, if they be growing there'; while the will drawn up in the following year by William Baker of Great Chishill in the far north-west of the county (now in south Cambridgeshire) left to Alice his wife 'the use of my twist [intertwined] walnut tree in my garden', and allowed her to take nuts from the orchard and to 'choose 2 of the apple trees in my orchard and gather the apples'. She also received '1 hive of bees standing in my orchard….'. As elsewhere, orchards might be grazed—although generally not by cattle or horses—and mown for hay. The will of Margaret Haward of Writtle, widow, of 1729 refers to apples, walnuts and plums in the orchard, and to 'one hay cock' standing there. The larger houses in the county's principal towns also had their orchards: a map of Chelmsford, surveyed in 1591, shows numerous examples. These early orchards generally appear to have been used to produce fruit for home consumption, with some surplus for the market. By the eighteenth century, however, there are signs of commercial specialisation, especially in the south of the county where fruit could be transported by boat up the Thames to London. In 1777, when a property in GraysThurrock called 'Ripleys, otherwise Notts, otherwise Stodies Farm' was placed on the market, the Great and Little Orchard together extended over no less than 18 acres (c. 7 hectares).

As in the other counties so far discussed, the scale of market production increased steadily through the nineteenth century, as the appetite for fruit grew in both London and in the main local towns, and as transport links improved. This was part of a wider development—the growth of the Essex market gardening industry— for many orchards formed only one part of a larger smallholding business. Essex market gardens grew celery, asparagus, radishes, onions and lettuces; the larger farms produced peas, cabbages, potatoes, cauliflower, carrots and early greens. Such enterprises were, unsurprisingly, concentrated in the south-west of the county, in the vicinity of London. But they were also prominent all along the band of light, well-drained soils which runs beside the Thames from Rainham to Stanford-le- Hope and Grays Thurrock. The latter parish had more than a fifth of its land area devoted to market-gardens and orchards by 1870.

The development of commercial orchards, and of market gardens, was accelerated by the agricultural depression of the late nineteenth century. Unable to make money from growing wheat, Essex farmers diversified their activities. The area devoted to orchards in the county almost doubled between 1871 and 1900, reaching a total of 2,521 acres (1,020 hectares). By this time there were around 4,000 orchards in Essex, significantly more than could be found in Hertfordshire to the west

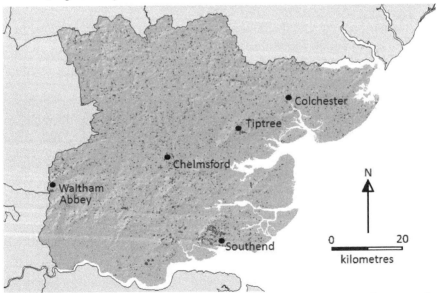

4.1 *The distribution of orchards in Essex in c. 1900. County boundary as it was in the nineteenth century.*

although, given the size of both counties, Essex had a rather lower average density. The Ordnance Survey maps produced around 1900 show that there were marked concentrations in the south of the county, especially in the area around Southend; a little further east, around Vange and Basildon; and in the Thurrock district. But there were also significant clusters around Brentwood, in the Lea valley between Waltham Abbey and Roydon, and in the vicinity of Tiptree (Figure 4.1).

This distribution largely reflects the presence of railways, roads or waterways which could move fruit easily to the London market, the proximity of large towns like Colchester, and to some extent the presence of relatively light, loamy soils. But it was also shaped by particular local factors. The cluster of orchards around Tiptree, for example, was associated with the jam factory which was opened in that village by Arthur Charles Wilkin in 1885. The family farm had begun to concentrate on the production of fruit two decades earlier, taking their plums and apples to Kelvedon railway station for transport to the London markets. Wilkin's move into jam production, in the form of the Britannia Fruit Preserving Company, allowed a far larger market to be accessed (the very earliest preserves produced by the company were sold to a merchant who shipped them to Australia). Initially the company faced

4.2 *Workers in the orchards of Wilkin and Son's jam company, Tiptree, in c. 1910.*

a number of problems, especially difficulties in attracting labourers to the factory, who reportedly objected to 'that funny work'. But by 1900 its orchards and small fruit grounds covered more than 800 acres (c.325 hectares) and were producing some 300 tons of fruit each season, including quince and medlar (Figure 4.2). This was not the only jam factory established in Essex in the late nineteenth century. Another was Elsenham Jam, based in the village of that name in the west of the county, not far from Bishop's Stortford. In 1890 a large fruit growing holding was established here by Sir Walter Gilbey, and Elsenham Jam registered as a company. It was taken over by Tony Blunt in 1959, when its product was advertised as 'the most expensive jam in the world'. The factory and offices were destroyed by fire in 1969.

The large orchards at Hadleigh, close to the Thames estuary, had very different origins. They were associated with something called the Home Farm Colony, which was established by the Salvation Army on the site now occupied by the Hadleigh Downs Country Park. In 1891 General William Booth purchased 900 acres (364 hectares), comprising Home Farm, Castle Farm. Park Farm and Sayers Farms, in the area between the village of Hadleigh and the estuary, with the intention of giving 'employment (and food and lodgings in return for his labour) to any man who is willing to work, irrespective of nationality or creed.' In less than a year 250 volunteers from the East End were working here. A few years later 450 men were being employed, and the writer Rider Haggard described how the colony was 'a place where broken men of bad habits, who chance in most cases to have had some connexion with or liking for the land, can be reformed, and ultimately sent out to situations, or as emigrants to Canada.' The colony had a diversified economy, with market gardens, livestock farm and a brickworks, but the orchards were particularly extensive, covering more than 20 hectares in 1900 and nearly 30 hectares by the 1930s. There was a jetty from which produce was taken by barge to London, although much of the fruit and vegetables was sold locally.

Through the first half of the twentieth century the number of orchards in the south and centre of the county continued to expand, as cereal production continued to bring in meagre profits, as the market for fruit grew inexorably, and as smallholdings proliferated, here as in other areas with County Council support. Some commercial orchards now appeared on the heavy London clays, on soils not particularly suitable for fruit production, especially around Southminster on the Dengie peninsula. Smallholders in particular exploited every opportunity to make money from their orchards. In 1900 James Taber Senior, of Little Braxted near Witham, recorded how he had put mistletoe on his apple trees in his new orchard, presumably to sell at Christmas time! Typical was a farm called Bovingtons in Hatfield Peverel, put up for sale in 1919 and described in the sales catalogue as a fruit, market garden and corn farm. It included 52 acres of young fruit trees—apples, pears and cherries —and fruit bushes. But many enterprises concentrated solely on fruit production, often combining orchards with fields of soft fruit like raspberries. A valuation made in 1932 of a 'farm of fruit trees' at Buttsbury Lodge, Stock, between Brentford and Chelmsford recorded 1,050 half-standard Worcester Pearmain apple trees, 155 half-standard Early Victoria (a variety of apple now known as Emneth Early) and 405 half-standard Newton Wonder. All had been planted in 1930 as three-year-old trees, and were together judged to be worth £483. They were accompanied by 19, 912 blackcurrant bushes, planted at the same time, valued at £284. The growth of orchards and fruit farms in the first half of the century was greatest in the area of the A12 'corridor', and particularly marked in the parishes of Hatfield Peverel, Boreham, and Terling, a few kilometres to the north-east of Chelmsford. In 1900 there were only scattered farm orchards in the area but by the 1940s vast acreages existed here, mainly planted by the Seabrook family of Boreham in the inter-war years. At its peak the firm had 1,150 acres (465 hectares) of orchard and nursery, and 200 full time staff, as well as part-timers—which might likewise reach 200 during the picking season.

Since the 1970s commercial orchards have been in steady decline in Essex. Some fine enterprises remain, often attracting custom by providing a wide range of fruit varieties, such as Crapes Fruit Farm in Aldham near Colchester (Figure 4.3), or Manor Grove Farm at West Bergholt. The orchards run by the Wilkin family around Tiptree continue to produce fruit, partly for jam and partly to supply shops. But most Essex orchards have been grubbed up, replaced by arable fields or, in districts where development

4.3 Crape's Fruit Farm at Aldham still sells a wide range of old fruit varieties.

pressures have been greatest, houses. The area around Southend-on-Sea—the parishes of Prittlewell, Leigh-on-Sea and Rayleigh—had vast numbers of orchards in the inter-war years, and substantial numbers survived into the 1960s. Today they have almost all been built on. St Laurence's orchard near the airport survives but otherwise, only small fragments remain. One example, suitably augmented by recent planting, survives on the central reservation of the A127, on the eastern side of Southend!

From the late eighteenth century small nursery businesses proliferated in the county, serving the growing numbers of commercial fruit growers. When Lawford Lane Nurseries at Writtle was put on the market in 1897 the property comprised

6 acres of pasture land and around 8 acres of nursery ground planted with '4000 apple, pear, plum and other fruit trees…'. But by far the most important nursery business was that of William Seabrook & Sons, based at Boreham. As already noted, the company—which was begun in the 1880s—were mainly commercial fruit growers, initially specialising in nectarines and peaches but, from 1886, branching out into apples, and gradually establishing a large number of orchards in Boreham and surrounding parishes. But they also introduced many new varieties, of apple especially, in the late nineteenth and the first half of the twentieth century, which they propagated and sold to other producers, and to the general public. The company published a book called *Fruit Production in Private Gardens* in 1942.

A large number of fruit varieties either originated in the county or are closely associated with it. The 'Tun Apple' is said to be have Essex origins—it is a rare eating variety, with a yellow skin and coarse, slightly aromatic flesh. Far more important is the Sturmer Pippin, a wonderful dessert variety (firm but juicy) which was first raised by the nurseryman Ezekiel Dillstone some time around 1800 in the village of Sturmer, near Haverhill on the boundary with Suffolk. Probably a cross of two long-established varieties, the Ribston Pippin and the Nonpareil, it is still often found in gardens and old orchards in Essex and adjoining counties—unlike the Waltham Abbey Seedling, raised at Waltham Abbey by John Barnard in 1810, which is now completely lost. Also widely found in Essex, and more generally across eastern England, is the apple known by the rather picturesque name of 'D'Arcy Spice' (Figure 4.4). This is traditionally said to have been discovered in the garden of Tolleshunt D'Arcy Hall near Colchester around 1785, but it may have earlier origins. What was probably the same apple was marketed by John Harris of Bromefield under the name 'Baddow Pippin' around 1848; and by Rivers' nursery, just over the county boundary in Hertfordshire, in the 1850s under the name 'Spring Ribston'. With its sweet, firm, rather aromatic flesh it is an excellent eating apple. The London Pippin, also known as the Five Crowned Pippin, is a very old late-keeping culinary apple which may also have been developed in Essex and was certainly widely grown here in the nineteenth century, although a Norfolk origin has also been suggested.

4.4 *D'Arcy Spice, one of the most famous of Essex apples.*

Most of the apple varieties which are known to have developed in the county are, however, associated with Seabrooks of Boreham. They were responsible for a long list of new eating apples, including Flame, raised in 1925; Seabrooks Red (1925); Garnet (1936); Amber (1936); Topaz (1936); Opal (1936); Pearl (1938); Acme (1944); and Eros (1947). They also produced cooking apples like Monarch (1888) and Excelsior (1921). The former was particularly successful. It was widely grown in the orchards of south and central Essex and was especially popular during the Second World War, as it is sweet when cooked and thus requires little sugar. Seabrooks also marketed, from 1945, the 'George Cave' apple, first raised by George Cave of Dovercourt in 1925 and one of the earliest maturing English varieties, in some years ready for eating by the end of July. Other commercial nurseries also contributed to Essex's long list of apples, most notably the firm run by Mr Thorington of Hornchurch near London, which produced Sunburn and Edith Hopwood in the 1920s. But perhaps the county's most successful apple is Discovery, which originated in 1949. It was discovered by Mr Dummer of Langham, growing from a Worcester Pearmain pip, and was marketed by Jack Matthews of Thurston. It was originally named Thurston August. The flesh, which can be flushed pink, has the strawberry flavour of its Worcester Pearmain parent. An early apple, it is best ripened on the tree and eaten just after picking, when it is crisp and juicy. It becomes 'woolly' very quickly once picked. Pears were a major crop in Essex in the nineteenth and twentieth century and a number of varieties were raised here, including Gansel's Bergamot, a cooking pear which probably originated at Donneland Hall near Colchester in 1768; and Johnny Mount Pear, an old variety also perhaps associated with the Colchester area.

Essex has a number of orchards which are open to the public (check websites for details) and which are well worth visiting. St Laurence Orchard near Southend Airport is a 0.4-hectare remnant of a larger orchard, which was first planted around 1920 with Bramley's Seedling and King of the Pippins apple trees, some of which still survive amongst newer plantings. It is a survivor of the many orchards which could once be found in the district. Other collections, entirely of recent planting but now maturing, include those at Broadfields Farm, Pike Lane, Cranham near Upminster (part of the Thames Chase community woodland), which was planted in 1995 with an impressive range of apples and pears associated with Essex; and at Cressing Temple, planted 1993, where most of the county's varieties can be seen. At Audley End House, in the north-west of the county, the kitchen garden has been restored and planted by Garden Organic (and subsequently managed by English Heritage) with a wide range of old varieties of apple, plum and pear, with many of the trees trained or 'espaliered' against the walls, providing not only a rich harvest of fruit but a spectacular display of blossom in the spring. Lastly, the Jam Museum at Tiptree is well worth a visit. Here you can learn about the history of the Wilkin family and the business they ran, and see the old mulberry, medlar and quince orchards, as well as a new orchard planted with 6,000 fruit trees, representing many old varieties of apples, nuts, cherries and pears (Figure 4.5).

4.5 The Wilkin's Company orchards at Tiptree in Essex.

Recipes

Autumn Fruit Salad (serves 6)

As noted above, the apple called Discovery dates from 1949 and is an early variety, best eaten just after picking. In this condition, it is ideal for this recipe, although other dessert apples can of course be substituted. Try D'Arcy Spice or, if this cannot be obtained, Cox's Orange Pippin or similar.

Ingredients

450 g / 1 lb dessert apples

300 g / 10—11 oz blackberries

A couple of tablespoons of demerara sugar

1 lemon, zest and juice

2 tablespoons of an apple aperitif such as Somerset Pomona, or use a dry cider or cider brandy

Method

Zest and juice the lemon. Do not peel the apples. Core and chop them roughly and put in a decorative glass bowl with the lemon juice.

Toss the pieces of apple carefully in the lemon juice (to prevent them

4.6 Autumn Fruit Salad. Discovery, or D'Arcy Spice, are both excellent Essex varieties to use in this recipe.

browning).

Carefully mix in the blackberries and lemon zest. Sprinkle in the sugar and Pomona. Mix carefully. Chill. Serve with Greek yoghurt.

(Variation: try adding dessert pear, treated in the same way as the apple).

℘℘℘

Apple, Goat's Cheese and Cobnut Salad (starter, serves 6)

This is a modern recipe for a refreshing and light starter.

Ingredients
1 ½ D'Arcy Spice apples, or any other dessert variety with a firm, crisp texture and slight acidity. Try Sturmer Pippin or a Cox-type variety. For an early variety, when the cobnuts will also be in season, choose Discovery or George Cave

4.7 *Apple, Goat's Cheese and Cobnut Salad.*

1 ½ chevre blanc or similar cheese

75 g green cobnuts—they have a short season but will keep for a while in the fridge. Do not be tempted to freeze them, as this affects their texture. If not in season use whole dried hazelnuts, preferably with the inner skin still on

¾ bag salad leaves

1 teaspoon wholegrain mustard

Sea salt: Maldon would be a good Essex choice!

Freshly ground black pepper

1 clove garlic, crushed

2 tablespoons rapeseed or groundnut oil

2 tablespoons hazelnut oil (if you have any problems sourcing this try virgin rapeseed oil, which has quite a nutty flavour. Do not be tempted to use walnut oil as an alternative as its flavour is too overpowering)

1 tablespoon cider vinegar

Method
First make the dressing. Mix the mustard, salt, pepper, garlic, oils and vinegar. Whisk together or shake in a screwtop jar.

Core but do not peel the apples. Quarter and then cut each of the quarters into 3 slices.

Toss the apple slices in the dressing to stop them going brown. Cut the cheese into small pieces.

To assemble the salad, first arrange a handful of salad leaves on each individual plate. Then place 3 apple slices on the salad leaves and scatter with the cheese and nuts. Lastly, drizzle the rest of the dressing over the leaves and around the plate. Serve with seeded wholemeal bread.

(Variation: try using blue cheese and walnuts instead of the goat cheese and cobnuts, with walnut oil and apple balsamic (if available) or cider vinegar. If you want to avoid using nuts altogether try using Egremont Russet apples, which have a nutty flavour, and a rapeseed oil and cider / apple balsamic vinegar dressing).

🅂🅁🄲🅁

Apple Fritters

Apple Fritters in this country have a long history. The following recipe appeared in *The Forme of Cury* (the oldest surviving English cookbook, dating from around 1390).

> Frytour of pasternakes, of skirwittes, & of apples. Take skyrwittes and pasternakes and apples, and perboile hem. Make a batour of flour and eyren; cast therto ale and yest, safroun & salt. Wete hem in ye batour and frye hem in oile or in grece; do therto almaund mylke, & serve it forth.

This recipe is for parsnip (pasternakes) and skirret (a medieval root vegetable), as well as apple fritters. Almond milk was eaten on non-meat and fast days as a non-dairy alternative to cream.

Another recipe, this time from around 1450, appears in the British Museum's Harleian Manuscript 4016.

> Take yolkes of egges drawe hem together through a streynour, cast there-to faire floure, berme and ale; stere it togidre til hit be thik. Take pared appelles, cut hem thyn like obleies, ley hem in the batur; then put hem into a ffrying pan, and fry hem in faire grece or butter till they be browne yelowe; then put hem in dishes, and strawe Sugur on hem ynogh, And serve them forthe.

'Barm' is 'ale-barm', yeast taken from the surface of the ale during brewing.

This is a modern version of the recipe.

Ingredients
3 or 4 dessert apples, depending on size. The classic Essex varieties, D'Arcy Spice or Sturmer Pippin, would be ideal

1 egg

125 g / 4 oz plain flour

150 ml / ¼ pint / 5 fl oz light ale or dry cider

Pinch saffron (grown in Essex at Saffron Walden for several centuries), ground

1 tbsp caster sugar

Oil or lard for deep frying

Method
Sift the flour into a bowl and add the saffron.

Make a well in the centre and add the egg.

Beat the flour into the egg, adding the ale or cider gradually until you have a smooth batter. Leave for at least 30 minutes.

Peel the apples and cut them into slices 5 mm / ¼-inch thick. Dip into the batter and deep fry in the oil or lard at 180°C for 2—3 minutes until golden brown. Leave to drain on kitchen paper, then place in a serving dish and serve sprinkled with the sugar.

₭₨

Roasted Root Vegetables with Pear

This is a modern recipe for winter. It is a good way of using cooking pears such as Gansel's Bergamot, or any warden-type pear (see Bedfordshire).

Ingredients
A selection of root vegetables—red onions, potatoes, celeriac, turnips, parsnips, carrots, beetroot, Jerusalem artichokes etc (whatever is in season, and you have to hand).

Hard cooking pears.

Rapeseed oil

Freshly ground black pepper

Cloves of garlic, whole

Method
Preheat the oven to Gas Mark 6 / 200°C / 180°C Fan.

You will need 1 or 2 large baking trays—you will need to spread the vegetables out to cook in a single layer.

4.8 Roasted Root Vegetables with Pear.

Prepare the vegetables according to type. Peel all the vegetables apart from the potatoes, pears and garlic. Halve or quarter the onions, depending on size. Cut the vegetables into approximately 3 cm / 1 ½ -inch cubes. Halve, quarter, then core the pears. Cut into pieces the same size as the vegetables. Dry all the pieces with kitchen paper, then toss all the vegetables, pear and garlic in the oil and season with the black pepper. Spread them out on the baking tray/s. Place in the oven and cook, turning from time to time until browned ----- about 40 minutes. Add salt just before serving.

This is good on its own topped with crème fraiche, or served with roast pork or sausages.

(Variation: try adding smoked paprika, roughly crushed cumin and coriander seeds, or rosemary and thyme leaves to the rapeseed oil).

ଛଠଗ

Preserving Quince and Medlar

In the medieval period eating fruit and vegetables raw was regarded with suspicion and considered to be injurious to health. Recipes for preserving and cooking fruit therefore abounded, although the former also reflect the fact that most types of fruit were only in season for a short time. The following two recipes are from Hannah Woolley's *The Queen-like Closet OR Rich Cabinet* 1670. Hannah Woolley was married to Benjamin Woolley, schoolmaster for a time at the Free Grammar School in Newport near Saffron Walden. Both recipes are for preserving more unusual orchard fruits—quince and medlar—both of which are currently grown in the orchards of Wilkin and Sons of Tiptree, famous for their jams and preserves.

To make Cakes of Quinces.

This is a recipe for Quince Paste (like the Spanish membrillo) which is the forerunner to our modern marmalade. This was a sweetmeat with medicinal properties.

> Take the best you can get, and pare them, and slice them thin from the Core, then put them into a Gallipot close stopped, and tie it down with a Cloth, and put it into a Kettle of boiling water, so that it may stand steddy about five hours, and as your water boils away in the Kettle, fill it up with more warm water, then pour your Quinces into a fine hair Sieve, and let it drain all the Liquor into a Bason, then take this Liquor and weigh it, and to every pound take a pound of double refin'd Sugar, boil this Sugar to a Candy height, then put in your Liquor, and set them over a slow fire, and stir them continually till you see it will jelly, but do not let it boil; then put it into Glasses, and set them in a Stove till you see them with a Candy on the top, then turn them out with a wet Knife on the other side upon a white Paper, sleeked over with a sleek-stone, and set them in a Stove again till the other side be dry, and then keep them in a dry place.

To preserve Medlars.

Medlars are a strange-looking fruit resembling a cross between a small russeted apple and a rosehip. They are mentioned in Shakespeare.

> Take them at their full growth, pare them as thin as you can, prick them with your Knife and parboil them reasonable tender, then dry them with a Cloth, and put to them as much clarified Sugar as will cover them; let them boil leisurely, turning them often, till they have well taken the Sugar, then put them into an earthen Pot, and let them stand till they next day, then warm them again half an hour; then take them up and lay them to drain, then put into that Syrup half a pint of water wherein Pippins have been boiled in slices, and a quarter of a Pound of fresh Sugar, boil it, and when it will jelly, put to it the Medlars in Gallipots or Glasses.

Norfolk
Home of the Biffin

NORFOLK was for centuries a county of small farm orchards (Figure 5.1). They loom large in medieval documents: in 1386, for example, John Coppyng granted William Draper a 'Messuage and 12a., with buildings, orchard, hedges...' in Hockering; at Great Melton in 1391 there is a reference to a tenement with 'orchard and garden'; while at Long Stratton in 1505 there was a property called '...Geryesgardine, lately planted with fruit trees'. Leases, sales particulars and wills from the sixteenth, seventeenth and eighteenth centuries often refer to orchards, and some examples were described—often in considerable detail—by their owners. In 1734 Mary Birkhead laid out a new orchard, containing 44 trees, at her daughter's property in Thwaite St. Mary, some ten miles (16 kilometres) south of Norwich, describing it as 'an acre of land very near square'. The trees were planted in a grid—'in rows look which way you please'—and spaced '36 foot one way and 26 the other'. Most of the trees were apples and pears but the inside of the orchard's perimeter fence was planted with filberts, walnuts, several sorts of plum, quinces, and barberries. Mary's own orchard, also in Thwaite, was rather larger. It contained 152 trees, with a mixture of pears and apples planted in rows forming the main part of the plot, and with filberts, walnuts, cherries and plums again planted around the margins.

In addition to orchards attached to farms, documents suggest that even the gardens of most cottages contained a few fruit trees, often provided by landowners and clergy as an act of charity. In 1736, for example, the agent of the Marsham estate was ordered to buy '6 aple trees & 2 cherry trees to set in Ann Watsons yard & 2 apel trees in Jexes orchard at 8d a piece'. Fruit and nut trees were sometimes even planted in churchyards for the use of the poor, as at Briningham in 1750, where a number of walnut trees were established. The importance of fruit in the local economy is clear from the fact that they featured as elements in rental payments as late

5.1 An old farm orchard near Wymondham in Norfolk, planted shortly after 1900.

as the eighteenth century: in 1701 part of the payment for a piece of land in Downham Market in the west of the county comprised '3 lbs. potatoes and the fruit of three fruit-trees each year to Thomas Buckingham and his wife for their lives'. Most of the county's towns were also filled with orchards. Thomas Fuller famously declared in 1682 that it was impossible to tell whether Norwich itself was 'a city in an orchard or an orchard in a city', so full was it of fruit trees.

Such urban or suburban orchards were often under-planted with soft fruit. A lease for land in Heigham in Norwich from 1684 described it as being 'in form of a triangle planted with 60 fruit trees and 200 gooseberry and currant bushes'. Most of the county's early orchards, however, contained pasture between the trees, which as elsewhere was either grazed or cut for hay. The tithes paid each year on the latter are often recorded, as for example at Shotesham in 1649, where George Gooch paid a shilling for tithe hay in his orchard. Not only sheep but also pigs might be kept there, presumably ringed to stop them damaging the trees. In 1612 a property in Diss was conveyed 'with part of an orchard or hogs' yard'. This was common practice: three centuries later the Chivers company in Cambridgeshire were still keeping pigs in their orchards, something which helped fertilise the soil and reduce insect pests (it was claimed in the past that the pigs called Gloucester Old Spots got their spots from bruising caused by falling apples!).

Yet while orchards could be found everywhere in the county, by the end of the nineteenth century Norfolk—in common with Suffolk—displayed a marked

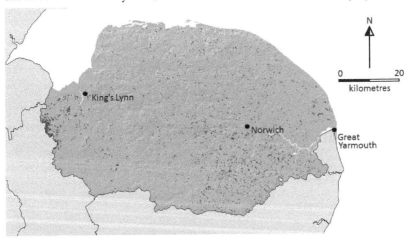

5.2 The distribution of orchards in Norfolk in c. 1900. The greatest density was in the Fenlands, in the far west of the county, where a major fruit growing industry had developed by the eighteenth century. Farmhouse orchards abounded on the claylands in the centre and south of the county, but were much thinner on the ground on the lighter soils in the north and west. County boundary as it was in the nineteenth century.

contrast between the heavier and more fertile soils, mainly concentrated in the south and east of the county, where almost every farm had its orchard; and the lighter and rather poorer land of Breckland and the north-west, where they were noticeably thinner on the ground (Figure 5.2). To some extent the suitability of soils for fruit growing may explain this variation, but for the most part it seems to reflect social and economic differences. Small farmers were especially numerous in the south and east, many of them owner-occupiers, and for such people orchards provided a useful additional income stream, as well as a source of nutrition for themselves and their families. Breckland and northwest Norfolk, in contrast, were districts of great estates and large tenant farms. Some of the latter extended over 500 acres (200 hectares) or more; they were occupied by well-to-do 'gentleman' farmers and run, in effect, as industrial grain factories. Such individuals had a more single-minded focus on arable production, and the fact that they held their farms on relatively short leases provided little incentive to plant fruit trees, which took several years to mature.

Although the largest estates—focused on great houses like Holkham or Houghton—were concentrated in the north and west of the county, large landed properties could be found to some extent almost everywhere, except perhaps in the wetlands of the Norfolk Broads in the east, and the Fenlands of the far west. Norfolk, more than the other eastern counties, is still notable for its great estates and country houses. These, as elsewhere in eastern England, were well provided with fruit trees, in orchards and gardens. A gentleman's fruit collection was an important part of the social landscape, and much correspondence was devoted to discussion of orchard plans and fruit varieties and suppliers. Gifts of fruit or fruit trees were often sent over considerable distances to family members and friends, or to impress social superiors. William Gunn of Smallburgh made many such gifts to colleagues and family members, as in 1807 when he despatched to Thomas Hearn of Buckingham 'some beefing plants, Ribstone pippins, and another non-pareil called the Summer, with instructions for planting'. Most country house gardens and orchards could boast large numbers of fruit trees, of many different varieties. The fruit trees ordered for the new gardens at Ryston Hall in 1672 included 24 varieties of apple and 18 of pear. Over two centuries later Benjamin Stimpson of Sall Moor Hall planted a new orchard, containing 219 apple trees, 29 varieties in all; ten plums, in five varieties; and other fruit. The clergy, too, were avid collectors. A valuation of Kettlestone Rectory made in January 1800 recorded 90 trees in the orchard, including 35 different varieties of apple and 7 of pear, along with cherries and plums. Several of the county's country houses still retain impressive collections of trees (Figure 5.3).

Fruit trees were enjoyed for their blossom as much as for their fruit and orchards were valued as ornamental as much as functional elements in the gardens of great houses. At Stiffkey Hall on the north Norfolk coast in the 1570s the orchard was 'pared' to create allees with paths of sifted gravel, while at Stow Bardolph in 1712 the 'wilderness' or ornamental woodland in the grounds was planted with '14 pears, 14 apples, 14 plums, 7 cherries all for standard trees'. A map of Channonz in Tibenham, surveyed in 1640, shows the orchard in

5.3 Fine old apple trees growing in the walled garden in the grounds of a large Norfolk country house.

a separate moated enclosure, adjoining that on which the mansion itself stood. Sixteenth- and seventeenth-century writers often recommended surrounding the orchard with ditches or a moat which 'will afford you fish, fence and moisture to your trees; and pleasure also' (Figure 5.4).

By the second half of the eighteenth century a major commercial fruit-growing area had developed in the flat Fenlands in the far west of the county, which extended across the county boundary into the adjacent parts of north

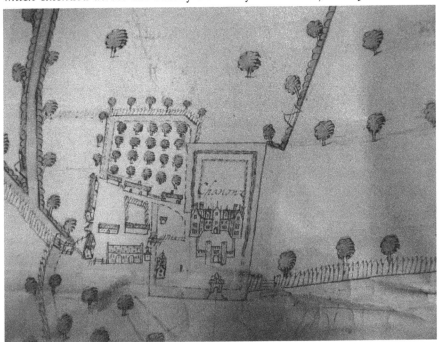

5.4 Channonz, Tibenham, in Norfolk, as shown on a map of 1640. The hall stands on a moated site, its orchard within a separate but connected moat.

Cambridgeshire. Already, by the 1840s, orchards covering 10 acre (c. 4 hectares) or more were relatively common in the district. Much of the fruit was shipped along the local waterways and thence along the River Nene, or around the coast via Sutton Bridge, to distant markets. The arrival of the railways in the 1850s, and the ease of transportation which they provided to the expanding towns and cities in the north and the

5.5 A train on the Wisbech and Upwell 'Tramway', photographed in the 1940s or 1950s.

Midlands, encouraged further expansion. So too did the agricultural depression which began in the late 1870s, which induced farmers to get out of the cultivation of wheat and potatoes, for which the rich silt soils had previously been farmed. It was partly to serve the orchards of the area that the Wisbech and Upwell 'Tramway' was opened in 1883. The light trains could stop and pick up goods anywhere on the line, making the line ideal for transporting fruit (Figure 5.5). By the 1930s the fruit-producing area in the Norfolk Fens was said to extend:

> From Upwell in the south to Terrington in the north, being about a mile in width in the south, it widens rapidly in the neighbourhood of Wisbech and exceeds 6 miles in the north at Terrington. The older orchards are to be found near Wisbech and the more recent extensions in the north, but so far the orchard area does not extend more than half a mile north of the Lynn-Sutton Bridge road. East of Terrington the continuity of the orchards is broken by grass and arable land, but there is a big concentration of orchards on both sides of the Great Ouse in the Wiggenhalls…

By this time, much of the fruit crop—mainly apples but including some plums—was tinned or otherwise processed locally, especially in Wisbech, just over the county boundary in Cambridgeshire.

The growth of the Fen orchards in the late nineteenth and twentieth century was accompanied by expansion elsewhere, especially on the loamy soils in the east of the county. This was part of the more general growth in market gardening and related activities encouraged by the continuing depression in agriculture and the expansion of markets afforded by widespread urbanisation, although here as in other counties it was also a consequence of government intervention. Norfolk County Council were amongst the most enthusiastic supporters of the County Smallholdings scheme, and by 1946 had 1,896 tenants in the county, occupying no less than 31,928 acres (12,921 hectares). In 1919 the County acquired the Burlingham estate in east Norfolk, which they divided into a plethora of smallholdings. Within a few years, orchards were thick on the ground here. Most have now gone, but one well-preserved example, probably established around 1925, seems to have been planted with a range of up-to-date varieties (Figure 5.6). What appear to be original trees include examples of Laxton's Superb (only marketed commercially from 1923); Golden Delicious (first marketed in England in

5.6 An orchard planted in the 1920s on one of the smallholdings created on the old Burlingham estate following its acquisition by Norfolk County Council in 1919.

the 1920s); Sunset (first developed in 1918); and Wealthy (first introduced from the USA in 1883 but only marketed on a large scale in the 1920s). All these were grown alongside longer-established varieties which had, by the twentieth century, become mainstays of commercial orchards, especially Robin pears, Cox's Orange Pippin, Bramley and Worcester Pearmain.

Although smallholders and small farmers were prominent in the expansion of commercial orchards in Norfolk, larger landowners—including members of the local gentry, responding to falling rent rolls and a depressed market for agricultural produce—were also active, creating large fruit farms in new areas. The Cubitt family had owned the Honing estate since the 1780s, and in 1907 began to plant an area of ten hectares immediately to the south of their park with fruit trees. This initial planting was steadily expanded over the following years—with a hiatus during the First World War—and by 1926 the Honing orchards covered more than 55 hectares in two main blocks. A wide range of apples was cultivated—Bramley, Lord Derby, Worcester Pearmain, Beauty of Bath, Court Pendu Plat, Queen, Lane's Prince Albert— as well as some pears, all interplanted with blackcurrants and gooseberries.

As in other parts of eastern England, orchards continued to expand in Norfolk through the 1940s, 50s and 60s, before beginning their long decline from the 1970s. Nevertheless, large areas remain under fruit trees in the Wisbech area, now the only major centre of fruit production in the region. Much of the industry is in the hands of large companies like Newton Fruit Farms or Mackle Apple Farms, but many smaller producers remain active, generally marketing their fruit through cooperatives such as Fruitlink. Bramleys have long been the most important crop, despite the fact that the variety had not originated in the region, but in the East Midlands town of Southwell in Nottinghamshire. Elsewhere in the county only a few commercial orchards survive, many catering for the 'pick your own' market and growing 'heritage' varieties, including Drove Orchards at Thornham on the north coast (with 16 hectares growing over 160 varieties of apple) and Plumbe and Mauf's plum orchards at nearby Burnham.

For much of the twentieth century a high proportion of Norfolk's apple crop was bought by the Gaymer's cider factory. The Gaymer family began producing cider at Banham at the end of the eighteenth century—a newspaper advertisement from the Bury and Norwich Post for 26 May 1800 states that John Gaymer had inherited the trade secrets of his father-in-law Joseph Chapman, secrets which were 'the result of the last ten years practice and experience'. The same advertisement emphasised that 'the cydermaking business is carried on by the said John Gaymer at Banham aforesaid, by whom all orders will be thankfully received, and readily executed'. John's son William was described in 1846 as landlord of The Crown in Banham, 'cyder manufacturer' and farmer, and in 1854 as a 'victualler and cider manufacturer'. But it was his son, another William (1842-1936), who really expanded the business, building a new factory beside the railway station in the nearby town of Attleborough, which was equipped with its own siding. The company grew steadily over the following decades, producing for export as well as for home consumption, eventually employing more than 400 people. Apples were purchased from farms right across East Anglia, and in particular made much use of the 'bag apples' or windfalls from the Fen orchards, which were unsuitable for other purposes (cider makers in eastern England, unlike their more famous fellows in the west of the country, did not use special cider apples for brewing, but ordinary cooking and eating varieties). In some years fruit was also sourced from orchards in Devon and in 1903, when there was a particularly poor apple harvest, from as far afield as Canada. There were extensive orchards planted around the Attleborough factory—many residents of the town can still recall the magnificent sight of the trees in blossom—but these were mostly for show, a form of advertising. Most of the apples grown there were actually sold, for cooking or eating (Figure 5.7).

The Gaymer's site was bombed in December 1940: an incendiary landed in the paper store, leading to an extensive fire which damaged, in particular, the bottling machinery and filtration plant. After the War these facilities were rebuilt, and through the 1950s the firm flourished, and remained the largest employer in Attleborough. Its main lines—Two Star, Diamond, Gay Flag, Gay Sec and Olde English—were exported to east and west Africa, South Africa and the USA. But from the mid-1950s demand for cider gradually declined, and so too the company's fortunes. In 1961 it was purchased by Showerings of Shepton Mallet, producers of Coates Cider; they in turn were taken over by Allied

5.7 The Gaymers cider factory, beside the railway line in Attleborough, photographed from the air in the 1950s.

Breweries in 1968. There were further changes in ownership before the factory was finally closed in 1995. The site was sold and most of the buildings, including the chimney stack—a local landmark—gradually taken down. The orchards had already disappeared, grubbed up in the late 1980s to make way for industrial units, a housing development and playing fields.

Norfolk's traditional farm orchards grew a range of fruit but, in terms of commercial production, this was predominantly an apple county. There are no special kinds of Norfolk plum and while novel varieties of cherry were developed in the county this was only in modern times, at the John Innes Research Centre in Norwich. Norfolk is best known for its apples. Some have known origins, including 'Look East', a cross of Cox's Orange Pippin and Blenheim Orange, which was raised by Mr Ormonde Knight of Yaxham in the 1970s; Golden Noble, found and developed by the head gardener of the Stow Bardolph estate in the nineteenth century; or Hubbard's Pearmain, first marketed and probably raised by the famous George Lindley—writer and botanist—at his nursery in Catton in the 1790s. Cockett's Red, a small sharp late-season red apple, was apparently developed in the 1920s by Samuel Cockett in the Fenland village of Walsoken; it was, according to tradition, widely used to make toffee apples. Norfolk Royal, a crisp and juicy eating apple but with rather a greasy skin, was found growing at a nursery in North Walsham in 1908 and marketed from the 1920; while Norfolk Royal Russet, a 'sport' of the variety, is a crisp dessert apple with a superior flavour which was discovered by the Rev. C.E. Wright in his garden at Burnham Overy Staithe in 1983, and marketed soon afterwards by a Gloucester nursery.

Other Norfolk varieties have early or obscure origins, including Pine Apple Russet, Winter Majetin and Winter Broaden, all of which were being widely grown by the early eighteenth century. The excellent cooking apple called Dr Harvey may also have Norfolk origins, although this is debated; argument also surrounds the origins of Adam's Pearmain, a late dessert apple with a distinctive elongated shape and an aromatic, nutty flavour, although a Norfolk origin seems more likely than a Hertfordshire one (the variety, which was first described in the 1820s, was also known as a Norfolk Pippin).

Arguably the most famous Norfolk varieties are Emneth Early and Norfolk Beefing. The former is a culinary apple, developed around 1897 by William Lynn of Emneth near Wisbech by crossing Lord Grosvenor and Keswick Codlin. The origins of the Beefing are lost in the mists of time and, while very strongly associated with Norfolk, the variety may not have originated there. It is a tough hard cooking apple which will keep—on the tree if necessary—into the spring months (there is some dispute as to whether its name derives from 'Beau fin', implying a French origin; or, as maintained by Hogg in 1884, comes from the baked fruit's supposed resemblance to beef). It was recorded in a fruit list from Mannington Hall, the home of the Walpole family, in 1698. It was used in a number of special ways, some of which we describe below.

Most of the orchards in Norfolk which are open to the public were planted during the last few decades, many with the help, or at the active instigation, of the East of England Apples and Orchards Project (EEAOP), an excellent organisation which is based in the county. Examples at Coltishall and Carbooke, and at the restored County School Station at North Elmham, are all worth visiting (check websites for times and access). Of particular note is that at Gressenhall Farm and Workhouse Museum near Dereham. This is an old institutional orchard which in recent years has become home to a stunning collection of varieties originating in Norfolk (many grafted on to original Bramley's Seedling trees). Also well worth a visit is the orchard of local varieties planted in 2000 as part of the Burlingham Woodland Walks, on land owned by Norfolk County Council which—rather fittingly—once formed part of the smallholdings carved out of the Burlingham estate. It is open at all times, and located on the A47 between Norwich and Great Yarmouth.

Recipes

Biffins

The Norfolk Beefing is, as noted above, a particularly hard, long-keeping apple. Despite its rather attractive appearance it is not pleasant to eat raw, as its texture is rather dry and its flavour bland. However, when cooked in certain ways it becomes a real delicacy. It was used, most famously, to make 'Biffins' (confusingly, also another name for the variety). During the nineteenth century these were extremely popular—not least as a Christmas delicacy, as described by Charles Dickens in *A Christmas Carol*. They were a Norwich speciality, prepared by bakers in their ovens as they cooled after bread-baking. They were cooked whole and gradually flattened and dried; then packed in boxes layered with sugar and sent to London fruiterers, or by post as gifts. They are best made in brick ovens and changes in commercial oven technology contributed to their demise, although they were available commercially until the 1950s.

Esther Copley in *The Housekeeper's Guide or a Plain and Practical System of Domestic Cookery* of 1838 gives the following recipe for 'Dried Apples or Pears', citing Norfolk Biffins (Beefings) as the best apple to use (and for pears she suggests using 'the large baking pears', that is, wardens—see Bedfordshire).

Have a baking wire on short feet, on which lay clean straw, then the fruit, then another layer of straw; set them in a cool oven, and let them remain in four or five hours; then take them out, press them in the hand very gently, to get them as flat as possible, without breaking the skins; put them again in a cool oven. If this process is repeated three or four times, they will become as flat and as dry as those which are sold at a high price in the pastry-cook's shop. To do them properly, requires two or three days.

Similar descriptions appear in other sources. Eliza Acton, writing in 1845, also describes something called a 'Cottage Biffin', which was "much finer........ left more juicy but partially flattened'. The following is a combination of recipes for 'Commercial' and 'Cottage' Biffins. It works better in an oven powered by electricity rather than in one powered by gas, and even better in an Aga-type range—but would work best of all in a brick bread oven!

Ingredients
Norfolk Beefing apples

Method

Preheat the oven to 100°C / Gas Mark ¼. Place a wire cake cooling rack over a baking sheet. Then place a layer of clean straw over the rack.

Wash and dry whole unpeeled Norfolk Beefing apples and arrange them on the straw.

Bake for 5 hours.

Remove the apples from the oven and very gently flatten them in your hands taking care not to break the skins. Put them back on the straw, cover with more straw and return them to the oven. After another hour flatten a bit more.

They can then be weighted. Place a heavy baking tray over the top layer of straw and place weights on top.

Turn the oven off after a total of around 12 hours, leaving the biffins in the residual heat.

The resulting fruit is very moist, with a creamy texture and concentrated flavour which the famous fruit expert Joan Morgan describes as almost that of raisins and cinnamon. The biffins are not totally flat but flattened, brown and wrinkly.

5.8 *'Biffins'—the most famous apple dish associated with the county.*

Dried Apple Rings

Dried Apple Rings are a good way of preserving apples, and one which was particularly important during the wartime and post-war rationing period. This can be done in a dehydrator (in which case, follow the instructions that come with the equipment) but can also be achieved in a normal domestic oven.

Ingredients
The hardness of the Norfolk Beefing also makes it ideal for drying, but any other variety to hand will do perfectly well (including windfalls, although you will need to cut out any blemishes).

Method
Preheat the oven to 100°C / Gas Mark ¼.

Wash and dry the apples, then peel and core them. Slice them thinly (about 5mm)/ ¼-inch thick). Steep the rings for 10 minutes in approx 1 gallon / 4.5 litres water to which 1.5 oz / 40 g of salt has been added. The rings can then be threaded onto canes and balanced over a deep roasting tin, or placed in a single layer on a wire cake cooling rack, placed on a baking tray. Dry slowly in the oven. When ready they will feel like chamois leather.

Note: pears, halved or quartered, can be dried in the same way, spread on a rack as described above.

ഇഐ

Preserved Green Codlings

A codling or codlin is a specific type of apple, namely one that cooks down to a purée. Old cookery books from the seventeenth or eighteenth centuries tend not to use the word 'apple' but instead specify a 'codlin' or a 'pippin'. In botanical terms a pippin is an apple grown from a pip but in the culinary world it is a firm, crisp dessert apple with a certain amount of acidity, like a Cox's Orange Pippin.

Ingredients
This recipe is from Elizabeth Raffald's *The Experienced English Housekeeper* of 1769 and uses very immature codlins, picked when they are about the size of a walnut, along with their stalks and a leaf or two. Emneth Early, originally known as Early Victoria, is a classic small codlin and ideal for this recipe. But it is worth experimenting with other, very small and immature apple varieties, either culinary or dessert. This really needs to be done in June or July.

The fashion in the eighteenth century was for bright green preserves and pickles. This was often achieved by the use of chemicals such as the roach alum, as in the recipe below, but also by cooking in copper or brass pans, which resulted in the production of toxic verdigris. Do NOT try this at home!

Method

Raffald's recipe begins by placing the codlins in a brass pan of warm spring water, layered with vine leaves until the pan is full. It should then be covered tightly and the codlins softened slowly. The skins should then be removed.

Return to the now cold water with the vine leaves. Add a little roach allum and cook very slowly for 3—4 hours until green.

Drain.

Make a syrup with equal quantities of sugar and water, and add the codlins. Boil gently once every day for 3 days. Put in jars and cover. According to other sources, the taste (and presumably texture) resembles that of preserved ginger.

Smoked Mackerel, Apple and Walnut Salad (starter, serves 6)

Another modern recipe, designed around the Adam's Pearmain but excellent using any crisp dessert apple with some balancing acidity.

5.9 Smoked Mackerel, Apple and Walnut Salad.

Ingredients

1 ½ dessert apples

¾ bag of mixed salad leaves

2-3 fillets smoked mackerel, flesh flaked and skin discarded

Dressing:

1 teaspoon wholegrain mustard

Salt

Freshly ground black pepper

1 clove garlic, crushed

4 tbsps cold-pressed rapeseed oil

1 tbsp cyder, or if available, apple balsamic vinegar

Method
First make the dressing by mixing the ingredients in a screwtop jar.

Core but do not peel the apples. Quarter and then cut each of the quarters into 3 slices, or cut each quarter into small chunks. Place in a bowl and toss them in the dressing, in order to prevent them from browning.

To assemble the salad, first arrange a handful of salad leaves on each individual plate. Then place 3 apple slices on the salad leaves and scatter with pieces of the flaked smoked mackerel. Lastly, drizzle the rest of the dressing over the leaves and around the plate. (Should there be any dressing left over it will keep in the jar in the fridge for a few days). Serve with wholemeal sourdough bread.

₭℞

Waldorf Salad

This is a version of the famous salad invented at the Waldorf Astoria Hotel in New York in the 1890s. In its original form the salad consisted only of apples, celery and mayonnaise. Walnuts were added at a later date. This version uses a walnut oil and cyder vinegar dressing instead of mayonnaise making it lighter and more refreshing.

Ingredients
Firm, crisp dessert apples such as Norfolk Royal Russet (which has a russetted skin with a bright red cheek), Adam's Pearmain or a Cox-type apple

Celery, including the leaves, chopped

Walnut pieces

Dressing:

Salt

Freshly ground black pepper

Wholegrain mustard

A tasteless oil such as grapeseed or groundnut

Walnut oil

Cyder vinegar

Method

First toast the walnuts. Use a large frying pan over the hob. Have a non-metallic cooling plate ready. Over a medium heat, toss the walnut pieces in the pan, turning then frequently with a spatula.

When they start to go brown and you can smell them toasting, you will need to act fast as they can burn very easily. Tip them quickly on to the cooling plate in a single layer and leave to cool.

Next make the dressing. Place all the dressing ingredients in a screwtop jar. Proportions are a matter of personal taste but around 1/3 vinegar to 2/3 oil (half grapeseed, half walnut) works well, with approximately 1 heaped teaspoon of wholegrain mustard and a sprinkling of salt and pepper. Shake the jar to mix the dressing and put some in the bottom of a large salad bowl.

Roughly chop the apple, place in the bowl, and toss to mix.

Add the chopped celery and cooled toasted walnuts. Mix gently. Chill. This is a wonderful salad to serve with cold turkey and ham in the days following Christmas.

This salad will keep for a couple of days in the fridge.

5.10 *A new take on the famous Waldorf Salad. This has a walnut and cyder dressing, rather than one of mayonnaise.*

Suffolk
Gages, Cyder and Cobnuts

SUFFOLK, even more than Norfolk, was quintessentially a county of small farm orchards. At the beginning of the twentieth century almost every farm had one, at least those thickly scattered across the boulder clays occupying the centre of the county. Only in the relatively narrow strip of sandy soils running along the coast—the area traditionally known as the 'Sandlings' or 'Sandlands'—and in the far north-west, in the sandy district of Breckland—were orchards less frequent (Figure 6.1). In part this was simply because there were fewer farms or settlements on these poor soils; in part, perhaps, it was because their dryness and acidity were not conducive to the successful cultivation of fruit trees. But as in Norfolk it may also have been because the land on these poor, light soils was mainly owned by large estates, and held by large tenant farmers with little interest in planting orchards.

In Suffolk, as in other parts of eastern England, orchards and fruit trees were

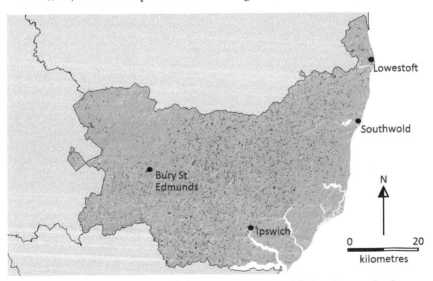

6.1 The distribution of orchards in Suffolk in c. 1900. As in Norfolk, farmhouse orchards were thick on the ground on the heavier clay soils, running in a broad band through the centre of the county, and less common on the lighter soils lying to either side. County boundary as it was in the nineteenth century.

for centuries a major part of economic and social life, and frequently referred to in deeds, wills, and legal agreements. A mid-thirteenth century document from Wortham in the north of the county even describes a rent paid in part with '1 apple annually at the feast of St Michael'. The formulaic wording of many leases and sales agreements suggests that no house of significant size lacked a collection of fruit trees. In 1656 a deed refers to 'three messuages, three gardens and three orchards....in Wetheringsett and Brockford'; another, from 1722, describes 'two messuages, two gardens, two orchards' in Bramford. Thomas Tusser, who farmed at Cattawade in south Suffolk in the middle of the sixteenth century and published his *Five Hundred Points of Good Husbandrie* in 1573, had no doubt of the importance of orchards to the farmer:

> Good fruit and good plenty doth well in the loft,
> Then make thee an orchard and cherish it oft.

A large number of farmhouse orchards still survive in the county, albeit often now incorporated into the gardens of what are usually no longer working farms (Figure 6.2).

In addition to farms, the manor houses and stately homes of Suffolk all had their orchards, and usually numerous fruit trees trained against the walls of kitchen gardens. It was at such places that the most extensive collections of fruit were to be found. When the Pines

6.2 An old farmhouse orchard in north Suffolk, partly incorporated into a garden. The magnificent tall, spreading tree is an old pear.

estate at Mettingham was put on the market in 1896 the orchard contained a phenomenal range of apples, the sales particulars listing specimens of: Waltham Abbey Seedling, Lord Suffield, Royal Somerset, Yorkshire Greening, Court Pendu Plat, Tower of Glamis, Northern Greening, Early Harvest, New Hawthornden, Cellini, Mere de Ménage, Easter Pippin, Normanton Wonder, Aromatic Russet, King of the Pippins, Kathleen Pippin, London Pippin, Nelson Codling, Gravenstein, Duchess of Oldenburgh, Cornish Gilliflower, Doctor Harvey, Crofton, Kentish Pippin, Bedfordshire Foundling, Yellow Joist, Philadelphia Pippin, Ribston Pippin, Golden Russet, Delaware Apple, Hubbard's Pearmain, Reinette du Canada, Flanders' Pippin, Pope's Apple, Lemon Pippin, Stirling Castle, Alfriston Apple, Harwell Souring, Court of Wick, Scarlet Nonpareil, Never Fail, Winter Non-Such, Scarlet Pearmain, Worcester Pearmain, Golden Winter Pearmain, Knobby Russet, Rymer, Norfolk Beaufin, Harvey's Wiltshire

Defiance, Blenheim Orange Pippin, Forge Apple, Striped Beaufin, Beauty of Kent, Pomona, Golden Harvey. There was also an impressive range of pears, including Fondante d'Automne, Duchesse d'Angoulême, Marie Louise, Beurré Diel, Comte de Lamy, Louise of Jersey, Williams' Bon-Chrétien; as well as plums and greengages! And in Suffolk, as elsewhere, local landowners also regularly provided fruit trees for the gardens of the poor. In October 1834 the noted horticulturalist Andrew Knight sent Lord Bristol of Euston Hall eighteen 'very little pear trees, which I will request you to give to your Cottagers to plant in their gardens, being confident that they will in a very few years, amply repay their care of them'. Arthur Young, writing in 1804, described how there was nothing about the orchards of Suffolk 'that seems to claim particular attention'. But, if unremarkable, the county's orchards were certainly ubiquitous, and deeply embedded in rural life.

Suffolk's distance from London ensured that it was less affected by the development of large institutions—with their associated orchards—than Hertfordshire or Essex. But there were some exceptions. One of the most notable was the 'Colonial College and Training Farm' at Hollesley Bay, on the coast some five miles from Woodbridge, established in 1887 to prepare young men for work in the colonies. In 1905 this became a centre for training unemployed Londoners in farm work, and then in 1938 a borstal institution housing 250 boys. By this stage, it had a farm of 1,600 acres (c. 650 hectares) attached, of which 300 acres (c. 120 hectares) were devoted to orchards and soft fruit. Distance from London, and from the industrial towns of the Midlands and the north, also discouraged the emergence of a major fruit-growing industry, of the kind exemplified, for example, by the south Bedfordshire 'prunes'. So, too, did the county's fertile soils and dry climate. Even in the agricultural depression of the late nineteenth and early twentieth century the county's farmers could generally make a good enough living from cultivating barley and, in particular, wheat, and had less incentive than their fellows in districts further south or west to lay down land for commercial fruit growing. Yet while large commercial nurseries never became a major feature of the Suffolk landscape in the way that they did, for example, in the Fens around Wisbech, at a local level some specialist fruit growers existed from an early date.

In the parish of Brent Eleigh, for example, Isaac Stansby owned two orchards in 1719, when he drew up his will, although this describes him only as a 'labourer', not a farmer. In 1726 he secured a mortgage of £10 from Robert Colman, a local gentleman, using for security the cottage in which he lived, 'with that part of the house inhabited by James Beeston and 2 orchards and all trees and water spring thereto belonging'. Whether because he defaulted on the payments, or for some other reason, a little later we find Stansby making a new boundary 'to separate that part of his orchard which he still possesses from part he now grants to Edward Colman, gent'. Small commercial orchards were especially common in and around the main towns, and often formed part of small market-gardening concerns, or grew soft fruit or nuts as well. In 1831 an inventory was compiled of the 'fruit trees of various sorts, currant and gooseberry bushes, nut bushes, etc etc' standing in a garden in Lower Olland Street in Bungay. It listed 678 plum, peach, apricot, nectarine, cherry, apple, pear and bullace trees, 37 nut bushes and 2,040 blackcurrant and gooseberry bushes. While mixed commercial orchards like this seem to have been the norm, there was some degree of local specialisation. The orchards around Stowmarket in the centre of the county, and those in the Sudbury district near the Essex border, were noted for their cherries, especially (in the latter case) a variety called the Polstead Black.

In the first half of the twentieth century the scale of commercial fruit production increased significantly in some parts of the county. Fruit growing was sometimes combined with other smallholding activities, such as poultry keeping. A sales advertisement from 1937 thus described a 'freehold grass orchards' in the parish of Nayland containing numerous apple, cherry and other fruit trees, a note at the end stating that 'The fowl house is not included in the sale'! Soft fruit were also grown, sometimes between the lines of orchard trees. In 1929 a property of 5½ acres at Bradfield St George was put on the market with a cottage, outbuildings, orchards and pasture land. The orchards were planted with about 450 plum, apple, pear, greengage, and cherry trees, together with 100 gooseberry and 2,000 blackcurrant bushes. By 1939 there were thought to be around 4,600 acres (1,862 hectares) of commercial orchards in the county, a figure which rose still further in the post-war years, peaking at 6,500 acres (2,630 hectares) in 1950. The main fruit grown were dessert apples, of which Cox's Orange Pippin were the most important, followed by Worcester Pearmain. Rather smaller numbers of cooking apples, mainly Bramleys, were cultivated; some pears; and a few plums. Orchards were generally more important in the east of the county than in the west, especially in the area between Woodbridge and Ipswich; they were to be found, according to a government report, 'on soils from sandy loams near the coast to heavy chalky clays inland with some on pockets of brick earth type south of Ipswich'. But it was only after the end of the War, in the 1940s and 50s, that really large fruit-growing concerns emerged, the most extensive probably being Risby Fruit Farms, on the Higham estate to the west of Bury St Edmunds, which by the 1960s had orchards extending over no less than 1,000 acres (405 hectares). As elsewhere, fruit production declined dramatically from the 1970s, and only a handful of commercial orchards remain, including Boxford Fruit Farms, Williamson's of Bradfield Combust, and Braiseworth at Eye.

One important twentieth-century fruit-growing business was that established by Justin Brooke, from Devon, whose father George was a Victorian tea trader (hence Brooke Bond tea). He acquired Clopton Hall in Wickhambrook in the 1920s, with several hundred acres of land, which he initially ran as both a fruit farm and a dairying enterprise, making deliveries of milk and dairy produce as far away as Cambridge. After the Second World War he rapidly expanded the fruit-growing side of the business, planting up to 100 acres per year from 1944, mainly with standard commercial varieties—Bramley, Worcester Pearmain and Cox's Orange Pippin apples, Conference Pears and Victoria plums. But peaches, nectarines, apricots and figs were also grown. The fruit was shipped to London and Covent Garden from the station at Clare. Brooke had his own tree nursery and also wrote a number of books on fruit cultivation: *Peach Orchards in England; Peaches, Apricots, and Other Stone Fruit* and *Figs Out of Doors*.

Large-scale commercial orchards certainly developed in Suffolk, but on a more limited scale than in adjacent counties, and the county's history of relatively small-scale farm production is to some extent matched by the absence of nurseries developing new fruit varieties, comparable to Laxton's in Bedfordshire or Rivers' in Hertfordshire. Important nursery companies certainly existed in the county from an early date. In 1751 the nurseryman Timothy Coleman died but his son and widow advertised that they were continuing his nursery business at Long Melford, selling 'a choice collection of fruit trees and best stock propagated in the best manner consisting of about an hundred of sorts of fruit.... Standards of 5 feet to 8 feet to the head and dwarf trained of all sizes. ...'. Two years earlier, Thomas Woods had established the more important, and longer-lived, Wood's Nursery at Woodbridge, which survived for 150 years until, following the death of John Wood in 1897, the site was sold to Roger Crompton Notcutt, who had a few years earlier begun a career as nurseryman with the purchase of the Broughton Road nursery in Ipswich. Although a number of significant nurseries continued to flourish through the twentieth century, such as Wickhambrook Nurseries, Notcutts remained the dominant supplier of fruit trees. But the company, although innovative in other fields of horticulture, did not itself develop, and market, new types of fruit to any significant extent.

Those varieties of apple that originated in Suffolk generally arose as sports or seedlings in local gardens, often those of large landowners, or were developed by their head gardeners. 'Lady Henniker', for example, is an excellent dual purpose apple, which was discovered in 1873 by Mr Perkins, the head gardener at Thornham Hall (the seat of the Hennikers) as a seedling growing in the discarded waste from cider making. The cooking apple Lord Stradbrooke, similarly, was either found as a seedling or deliberately raised by the head gardener at Henham Hall, near Wangford, a Mr Fenn, some time around 1900. Apples with more lowly origins include St Edmund's Russet, also known as St Edmund's Pippin, which probably originated as a chance seedling recognised by a Mr Richard Harvey of Bury St Edmunds, was later marketed by the Kent nursery of Bunyard's, and is still often found in gardens and old orchards; or Maclean's Favourite, raised by a Dr. Allan Maclean of Sudbury around 1820, a late-keeping variety now very seldom found. In addition to these old apple varieties, a few were developed by local nurseries in the middle or later decades of the twentieth century, including Clopton Red, a heavy cropping, bright red dessert variety raised by Justin Brooke of Wickhambrook Nurseries in 1946 and marketed from 1961; and Honey Pippin, a cox-like variety from the same nursery developed in 1955. More recent still is the Suffolk Pink which, although it was only developed and marketed in the 1990s, is variously reported to have been found as a coloured 'sport' of Laxton's Fortune, growing in the Braiseworth Orchards near Eye; as a 'sport' of the New Zealand apple Gala, found at Earl Stonham; or as having originated in France!

Suffolk is, perhaps, more famous for its association with some important varieties of plum. Coe's Golden Drop, a fine dessert plum, was developed by Jervaise or Jarvis Coe, a nurseryman in Bury St. Edmunds, some time around 1800, and while never very widely grown in England—it needs a good, warm summer to ripen to perfection— it was being widely cultivated in California and other warm regions by the end of the nineteenth century. Coe also developed a culinary variety

6.3 *Greengages gained their English name from the Gage family of Hengrave Hall in Suffolk.*

called St Martin, now seldom grown. Much more important than these, however, is the greengage (Figure 6.3). A long-established tradition relates how, in the eighteenth century, one of the Gage family of Hengrave Hall, near Bury St. Edmunds, received a shipment of fruit trees from France which included the plum called Reine-Claude; authorities differ over precisely which member of the Gage family, but the horticulturalist Peter Collinson, who died in 1760, reported that it was Sir William Gage, and that the trees were obtained some time around 1725 (Sir William had close connections with France, and met his wife Mary at the court of the Dowager Queen Henrietta Maria at Germain-en-Laye). According to some versions of the story, Gage's gardener managed to forget the tree's true name and therefore named it 'Green Gage' in honour of his employer; but other versions, including that given by Collinson, simply say that the fruit was named after Sir William because he was the first to introduce it to this country. Either way, this delicious (but often poorly-cropping) plum grows more or less true from seed, was widely marketed, and is still grown in gardens and orchards throughout England.

Perhaps Suffolk's most important claim to fame in the world of fruit and orchards is that it is home to one of England's oldest cider makers. The Aspall Cyder company takes its name from the village of Aspall, just north of Debenham, and was established by Clement Chevallier, who moved here from the island of Jersey in 1722. A friend later described how 'coming out of a Cyder country, amongst other improvements of his estate he has been a great planter of Apples, many of them of the sorts in use for Making of Cyder in Jersey & has had a large Mill for that use brought from Hence & has I believe been at a great expense for becoming a large dealer in it'. Clement's account books and letters show that he was planting within a fortnight of taking up residence, using a number of Jersey varieties, such as 'Caply' and 'Gros Fretchian'. These sources also, however, reveal that he made much use of local fruit, grown on the estate or purchased from neighbouring farmers, not only while his new trees were maturing but also after that time. His account books and letters describe the transport of his stone milling trough all the way from Normandy, and they detail the construction of the 'cyder house' (converted from an earlier barn) in which it was housed, along with his cyder press and other necessary equipment. The mass of documents in the Aspall's archive tell us much else—about how Clement marketed and transported his cyder (Clement always spells his product with a 'y') and how much of it he made each year. Production rose rapidly, reaching no less than 7,827 gallons a year by 1731.

Cyder making, and apple growing, have continued uninterrupted at Aspall Hall ever since Clement's time, although it has waxed and waned in scale over the centuries. It declined to some extent during the nineteenth century, when the family concentrated more on their arable farming (they developed the famous 'Chevallier barley' in the 1820s, which produced yields around ten per cent higher than other contemporary varieties and which was particularly suitable for malting). Cyder production increased once again from the end of the nineteenth century, however, first as agricultural depression encouraged diversification into other activities, and more rapidly from 1908, with the arrival of a rail line in the neighbourhood and the construction of Thorndon and Aspall Station a little over a kilometre to the north of Aspall Hall. An article in the *Suffolk Chronicle and Mercury* for 1914 described how production had been 'very considerably augmented since the construction of the Mid Suffolk Light Railway', so that the

6.4 The cider mill, installed by Clement Chevallier in the 'Cyder House' in the grounds of Aspall Hall in 1722.

6.5 The apple orchards surrounding the Aspall Cyder company's factory at Aspall in Suffolk.

family had been induced to 'very considerably extend this phase of farming at Aspall Hall'. The company expanded more dramatically from the early 1970s, and has gone from strength to strength ever since, although the firm has recently been taken over by an American company. It is a remarkable story of persistence and continuity. Clement Chevallier's cyder house, with his original mill and press inside it, still survives near the hall, although now somewhat incongruously surrounded by modern steel vats and other plant. It is a precious piece of industrial archaeology, although not currently open to the public on a regular basis (Figure 6.4). The factory is still surrounded by apple orchards (Figure 6.5).

A number of community orchards have been planted in Suffolk over recent decades, at Debenham, Middleton, Leiston, St James South Elmham, Great Cornard, Clare and elsewhere; Ipswich has several (check websites for details). At Woodbridge a network of small 'scattered' orchards, each with a handful of trees, is being established. One of the most exciting projects currently underway is, however, the creation of a 'county collection' orchard at the wonderful Museum of East Anglian Life at Stowmarket, which will feature examples of all the fruit varieties associated with Suffolk.

Recipes

Greengages with Flaked Almonds and Amaretto (serves 4)

As noted above, the greengage is said to have got its English name from the Gage family of Hengrave Hall near Bury St Edmunds. Its French name is Reine-Claude (Queen Claude), after the wife of the sixteenth-century King François I. This dessert is very refreshing. Gages have an almost honeyed flavour, more intense than most plums.

6.6 *Greengages with Flaked Almonds and Amaretto, an excellent way of using a fruit with close associations with Suffolk.*

Ingredients

500g / 1 lb greengages

Demerara sugar to taste, perhaps 3 tbsps

Flaked Almonds, 2 tbsps

Amaretto, 3 tbsps

Method

Choose a decorative glass bowl. Halve and stone the greengages and place in the bowl. Add the demerara sugar and the Amaretto, and stir carefully to mix. Sprinkle the flaked almonds over the top. Chill until ready to serve. Mix again before serving.

Serve with double cream or Greek yoghurt.

This is a flexible recipe and can be made with any variety of plum or gage.

⋙⋘

Fruit Leather

Fruit leather can be made with any fruit, singly or in combination. A savoury version can also be made, using tomatoes. This is not a traditional English recipe; fruit leathers were made in this country in the past, but by a different method, and with a different result. Our traditional fruit leather was a fruit preserve, made by boiling fruit pulp / juice with an equal quantity of sugar. The resultant fruit paste or cheese was then partially dried. The fruit leather described here is a type developed in hotter climates and was originally left to dry in the sun. It results in a thin, very concentrated, semi-translucent sheet which can be cut into strips to put in children's lunch boxes. It can also be formed into a cone shape and used as a container for ice cream. This recipe uses Lady Henniker, a dual use apple originating at Thornham Hall. But you can experiment with whatever fruit you have to hand.

Ingredients
1kg Lady Henniker apples

Juice of a lemon (optional)

Honey to taste (also optional, though it should be noted that Lady Henniker is not a sharp apple)

Method
Prepare two 24x30 cm baking tins by lining them with baking parchment. Preheat the oven to 60°C. Peel, core and roughly chop the apples. Place in a heavy-based pan with a tablespoon or two of water (you can always add more if necessary but you don't want the resulting purée to be too liquid).

Cook gently, stirring frequently to prevent sticking and burning, until the fruit is very soft. Purée and then taste. Stir in honey if you are using it.

Spread the fruit pulp thinly and evenly over the baking parchment using the back of a spoon.

Place in the oven and leave for 12—18 hours (or longer!) until the purée is dry and easily peels off the baking parchment.

When cold, roll the fruit leather sheets in fresh baking parchment and store in an airtight tin. This will keep for some time (if you can resist eating it!).

This kind of fruit leather can also be made using a dehydrator. Follow the instructions that come with the equipment.

ഗ്രൂ

Nectarines or Peaches Poached in Dessert Wine (serves 4)

This recipe is a homage to Justin Brooke, whose Wickhambrook orchards grew both nectarines and peaches.

Ingredients
4 nectarines or peaches

Approx 375 ml sweet dessert wine (or use a dry white wine or rosé, and add 2 or 3 tbsps caster sugar, depending on the sweetness of the wine used)

Method
Preheat the oven to 190°C / Gas Mark 5.

Choose a shallow china ovenproof dish, large enough to take the halved fruit in a single layer. Halve the fruit lengthways: leaving the stones in one half will add to the flavour. Arrange the fruit, cut side up, in the dish. Pour over the wine so that it half covers the fruit. Cover with foil and bake for around 15—20 minutes, until tender when pierced with a skewer. Leave until quite cold, then cover and refrigerate until ready to serve. Serve with double cream.

(For a citrussy flavour and a delicate pink colour try adding a teaspoon or so of dried lavender).

This recipe can be used for any stone fruit.

ഗ്രൂ

Spiced Salted Cobnuts

Cobnuts—the larger, domesticated form of the hazel nut—were a common feature of traditional orchards, especially in Suffolk.

Ingredients
100g cobnuts, shelled weight

1 tbsp olive oil

6.7 Spiced Salted Cobnuts.

2 tsps fine sea salt

2 tsps ground cumin

Method

Have ready a non-metallic plate on which you have placed a double thickness of kitchen paper.

Put the oil in a large frying pan and add the cobnuts. Fry on a medium heat, moving them constantly with a spatula. You will need to watch them carefully as once they start to brown, they can burn very quickly.

When they are golden brown take them off the heat and quickly tip them on to the paper-lined plate. Arrange them in a single layer.

Sprinkle them with the salt and cumin. Leave them to cool. Most of the oil will drain into the paper. Serve with drinks. They will keep in a lidded container.

This recipe uses fresh green cobnuts so the result is not quite as crisp as it would be using dried nuts.

(Variation: this is a very versatile recipe. Experiment with different combinations of nuts and spices. Try almonds, cashews or walnuts. Try other spices, such as smoked paprika).

ഇരൻ

Red Cabbage, Apple, Celery and Cobnut Salad

The apple used here is Suffolk Pink but any crisp, juicy dessert or dual use apple with a balancing acidity can be used, such as Cox or similar. An apple with a colourful skin like Discovery (see Essex) would also be a good choice.

6.8 *Red Cabbage, Apple, Celery and Cobnut Salad.*

Ingredients

Half a medium-sized red cabbage, shredded

3 sticks celery, including leaves, chopped

3 medium-sized apples, as described above

2 salad onions, chopped

100 g shelled cobnuts or, if unavailable, use dried hazelnuts

Optional: some celery leaves to garnish

Dressing:
Salt

Freshly ground black pepper

Wholegrain mustard

Hazelnut oil if available (this can be difficult to source, in which case substitute with cold-pressed rapeseed oil—there are a number of rapeseed oils produced in the eastern counties)

One of Aspall's cyder vinegars

Method
Make the dressing first. Place all the dressing ingredients in a screwtop jar: proportions are a matter of personal taste but around 1/3 vinegar to 2/3 oil would be about right, and approximately 1 tsp wholegrain mustard for an average-sized jar, together with a sprinkling of salt and pepper. Shake to mix the dressing and then put some in the bottom of a large salad bowl.

Roughly chop the apple, put it into the dressing and stir to coat. This prevents the apple from browning.

Add the shredded red cabbage, chopped celery and leaves, chopped salad onion and shelled cobnuts. Stir gently to mix, adding more dressing if necessary.

Garnish with celery leaves (optional).

This salad will keep in the fridge for a couple of days. It is very refreshing and particularly good as an accompaniment to cold turkey and ham.

૪ળ૨

Blackcaps Par Excellence

Although this recipe is best made with Norfolk Beefing apples, it is included here for two reasons. Firstly Eliza Acton, on whose recipe (in *Modern Cookery for Private Families*, published in 1845) this is based, was brought up in Ipswich. Secondly, the liquid used is Aspall's Imperial Vintage no 289 Suffolk Cyder which, according to its tasting notes, has 'notes of raisins, dates and prunes': the original recipe used raisin wine. If Norfolk Beefing apples are unavailable, choose a variety such as Blenheim Orange.

Method

Preheat the oven to 220°C / Gas Mark 7.

Take a shallow non-metallic ovenproof dish. Cover the base with a thick layer of soft light brown sugar.

Do not peel the apples. Cut them in half horizontally and scoop out the cores (use a serrated grapefruit spoon if possible).

Fill the cavities with mixed peel, with some lemon zest added.

Press the two halves of the apples together and place in the dish on top of the sugar, with all the apples close together.

Pour over the cyder, making sure you moisten the tops of the apples. Then sift caster sugar thickly over the tops.

Bake for around 10 minutes, until the tops are very dark brown. Then reduce the temperature to 200°C / Gas Mark 6. Cook until the apples are tender when pierced with a skewer. This should take about 40 minutes but do check regularly. (Note that these cooking times are for Norfolk Beefing. For Blenheim Orange or other kinds of apple the cooking time will be rather less.)

Don't use a variety like Bramley which will 'collapse'. The apple needs to hold its shape.

6.9 Blackcaps Par Excellence.

Cambridgeshire
Orchard County

CAMBRIDGESHIRE is the final county to be discussed in this book, but in many ways the most important. In 1900 it contained more orchards than any other county in eastern England, far outstripping its nearest rivals. They

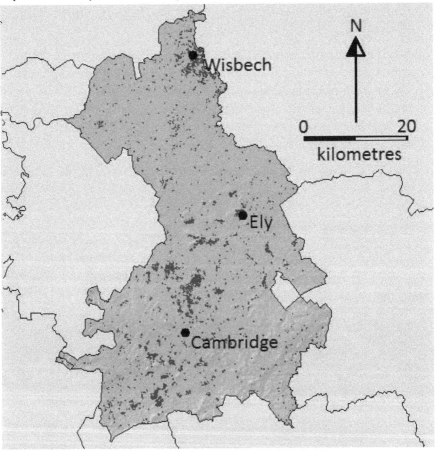

7.1 *The remarkable density of orchards in Cambridgeshire in c. 1900. The concentration in the far north of the county forms an extension of the Norfolk Fen orchards, centred on the town of Wisbech. Further south, a broad band of orchards runs along the southern margins of the peat Fens, with outliers on the Fen 'islands'—patches of higher ground—around Haddenham, Wilburton and Soham. A third concentration existed on the loamy soils in the far south of the county, where villages like Melbourn, Meldreth and Haslingfield had vast areas of fruit trees. County boundary as it was in the nineteenth century (and thus excluding Huntingdonshire).*

were clustered in three main areas (Figure 7.1). Firstly, there was a marked concentration in the far north of the county, on the silt Fens around Wisbech, which formed a continuation of the important fruit-growing district of west Norfolk which we have already noted. Secondly, orchards were numerous along the southern margins of the Fens, and on the various islands of higher ground within them, especially around Ely, Haddenham and Soham. The soils of the southern Fens were formed in peat, rather than in silts and clays, and made for poor fruit-growing country. Orchards were located on the higher and drier ground, especially on the well-drained soils around Willingham and Over. Lastly—and nearly, but not quite, merging with this—were the orchards on the loamy soils in the far south of the county, in villages like Melbourn, Meldreth, Haslingfield or Great and Little Eversden.

As elsewhere, small orchards attached to farms and manor houses had existed in Cambridgeshire for centuries, growing fruit for domestic consumption and a small surplus for sale, grazed by livestock and cut for hay. In the early years of the eighteenth century the rector of Fowlmere, in the south of the county, recorded in his accounts the payments made for cleaning the orchard pond, and to 'old Wil: Thrift for a day in mowing orchard and carrying out grass, though he could not be a day about it'. A survey of the Manor of Wilburton, drawn up in 1636, records 'the dwelling houses, orchards, gardens or yards in the Town with the number of acres, roods and perches that each of them contain'. Eighteen of the village farms, in addition to the manor house and parsonage, had an orchard; nineteen were described as having a 'yard' or 'homestead' only. Of course, it is unclear how 'orchard' is being here defined, and it is likely that the 'yards' and 'homesteads' themselves contained some fruit trees. Small orchards were thus a familiar feature of domestic life, in Cambridgeshire as elsewhere. But gradually, through the eighteenth and nineteenth centuries, fruit production in the county became more commercial in character.

The large orchards in the Fens and Fen Edge had already become a notable feature of the landscape by the end of the eighteenth century. In 1811 William Gooch described how in 'Ely, Soham, Wisbech &c.' there were 'many large gardens, producing so abundantly of vegetables and common kinds of fruit, as to supply not only the neighbouring towns but counties, the produce being sent to a great distance, to Lynn, &c. &c. by water, and by land, affording employ for many hands, labourers, retailers, carriers, &c. &c.'. He added that orchards were also 'numerous and large in the same districts as the gardens; the chief growth, apples and cherries ; Soham is remarkable for the latter.' Nevertheless, there was considerable expansion in the course of the nineteenth century, especially in the south of the county.

Expansion often followed hard on the heels of enclosure, which came late to many of the orchard villages: Haslingfield was enclosed in 1821, Orwell in 1837, Over in 1840, Melbourn 1839, Cottenham 1845, and Willingham as late as 1846. The small farmers in these places were already growing fruit on a semi-commercial basis in their crofts and gardens: this belated privatisation of the surrounding land saw a phenomenal expansion in their endeavours. But this would not have been viable without a way of transporting fruit to market, and here the arrival of the railways in the middle of the century was crucial. Most of the fruit growing villages in the county were located within five kilometres of a railway station. In addition, the great agricultural depression of the late nineteenth century encouraged smaller farmers, in particular, to diversify out of cereal growing, and into fruit production. But on top of all this the fruit growing industry was further stimulated by the establishment of the Chivers jam factory in Histon.

The Chivers family settled in the village some time around 1817 and initially made their living as farmers, growing wheat and barley. But in 1850 Stephen Chivers bought land beside the new Histon station, on the Cambridge-St Ives railway line, which had opened three years earlier, and planted some of it with fruit trees. The orchards were gradually expanded, reaching a total of 160 acres (65 hectares) by 1861. To begin with, much of the fruit grown was sent, via Cambridge, to the market at Covent Garden in London, but Chivers was soon distributing it more widely, and especially in the north and the Midlands. In 1870 he established a distribution depot, under the control of his sons William and John, in Bradford. According to family tradition, much of the fruit sold there was purchased by local jam makers, and the two young men persuaded their father that the family would make more money if they did this themselves, transporting the finished product, as it were, rather than the raw materials. Accordingly, in 1873 the first Chivers jam was produced in a small barn and two years later the Victoria Works was erected on the orchard site, beside the railway and equipped with its own sidings (Figure 7.2). Initially the jam was put into stone jars but in 1885 the first glass jars came into use. Other forms of processing soon followed, with marmalade, fruit jelly, lemon curd, mincemeat and Christmas pudding all being produced by 1895. In 1894 the first canned fruit in England was being sold by the company. By this time the company owned some 300 acres (c. 120 hectares) of orchards in the parish and had over 400 regular employees, a number bolstered by seasonal workers during peak times. By 1900 a substantial new factory had been erected, equipped with the first automatic canning machinery in Europe, designed by the firm's engineer Charles Lack. He also developed a range of processing and sterilising equipment. H. Rider Haggard visited in 1902 and described how 'The factory with its silver

7.2 Chivers Jam factory at Histon in Cambridgeshire, c.1890.

lined boilers, its cooling rooms, its patent apparatus for filling jars, its tramways, its printing and silver plating packing case making, labelling, baking powder, mincemeat and lemonade departments etc. was a truly wondrous place.'

The firm expanded steadily following its incorporation as a public company in 1901, exporting on a large scale, and by the 1920s the main processing buildings, fruit stores and ancillary buildings sprawled over an area of more than 7.5 hectares. The factory had its own water supply, produced its own electricity and manufactured its own cans. It featured a paint shop, sawmill, smithy, carriage works and barrel making workshop. By 1931 some 3,000 people were employed at the Histon works, and other factories had been opened at Huntingdon, and in Montrose and Newry. Chivers was by now the largest canner of fruits and vegetables in England. The factory's presence provided further strong encouragement for fruit-growing across Cambridgeshire. The Chivers family business was an integrated one. The farms also produced livestock: chickens ranged freely in the orchards, eating insect pests and fertilising the soil. Their eggs were used in the production of lemon curd and mayonnaise. Pigs were also kept in the orchards, also fertilising the soil.

A complex range of economic and technological factors, combined with the suitability of local soils and climate for fruit production , thus ensured that orchards expanded steadily in Cambridgeshire through the second half of the nineteenth century, and into the first decades of the twentieth. Already, by 1900, they occupied nearly a tenth of the land area in parishes like Little Eversden or Meldreth. In many cases, and probably to a greater extent than in other counties, soft fruit was cultivated between the rows of trees. Typical was a property in Ely which was advertised for sale in 1880, described as a:

> Fertile and productive garden ground, in a high state of cultivation, planted with a choice selection of apple, pear, plum, and other trees in full profit and bearing, and as undergrowth with gooseberry and current bushes, which produce large quantities of Fruit for the London and Manchester markets.

Many of the orchards in the south of the county, like this one, grew plums, usually although not invariably alongside apples and some pears. In 1889 the crops in four orchards at Meldreth were auctioned: one was said to contain 'greengages and other plums', pears and apples; another, 'principally greengages and damsons'. Towards the north of the county the emphasis was more on apples and increasingly—from the late nineteenth century—on cooking apples, especially Bramley's Seedling but also varieties like Lane's Prince Albert and Newton Wonder.

Fruit cultivation was often—as in other parts of eastern England—combined with market gardens and smallholdings. Typical was a 'productive and well-planted orchard with buildings thereon' in Ely which was placed on the market in 1913, complete with 'two piggeries, fowl house and lean to cart shed'. Kept for most of the time in sheds and sties, the manure from the livestock was easily collected and spread around the trees. The Ely property covered only 4 acres (c. 1.6 hectares) but larger fruit farms—with rows of trees usually inter-planted with soft fruit, cut flowers or vegetable—also existed. One in Willingham in 1935 covered 114 acres (46 hectares), with an additional 54 acres (22 hectares) of arable land: the orchards contained both apples and plums, in some cases planted in alternate rows. The owner had fallen into financial difficulties and a valuer's report described how 'with the object of reducing his Labour costs, he has allowed the whole of the orchard land to grass down and no longer cultivates the underlying land for bush fruit, or for such crops as potatoes, sugar beet etc. He has in fact concentrated on the top-fruit trees and these have been well pruned and regularly sprayed'.

The county's orchards at what was probably their peak were described by Pettit in 1941.

The small area of Greensand in the parish of Cottenham is remarkable for the intensive production of soft fruits, and of cutting flowers and vegetables. This type of cultivation showed an almost continuous increase in importance from the second quarter of the nineteenth century ..... Produce is marketed locally and to a factory at Histon [i.e., Chivers], in the Midlands and to a comparatively minor extent London.

He continued:

The most important top fruit is the plum, with the apple a good second and the rest "nowhere"... Interplanted arable orchards are the rule and intercultivation is carried a stage further in the production of cutting flowers and vegetables.

Of course, not all the county's orchards were commercial concerns, or were associated with farmhouses. As elsewhere, in the period before the twentieth century fruit trees were sometimes planted in the cottage gardens of the poor, or for their use in churchyards: a walnut, a pear and four plum trees were thus planted on the south side of Harston churchyard in

7.3 The orchard at Girton College, Cambridge.

March 1800. Great country houses like Wimpole Hall had their orchards and fruit grounds, as did some institutions like mental hospitals. The grounds of the older Cambridge colleges were often too cramped for extensive orchards, although fruit trees often featured prominently in the Fellows' Gardens, but those occupying more spacious sites, such as St John's, possessed them. The only large surviving example is at Girton College, an institution which was founded initially in Hitchin in 1869, moving to its present site on the outskirts of the city in 1873. The orchard was apparently planted a few decades later (it is first mentioned in the college records in 1904), covered a little under 2 acres (c. 0.8 hectares) and contained over a hundred trees (Figure 7.3). According to college tradition, it was established by Elizabeth Welsh, Mistress between 1885 and 1903. Some survivors of the original planting remain. They include pears and plums but are mainly cooking apples which were used in the college kitchens. There are also ancient quinces and a remarkable walk along the north side of the orchard which is lined with honeysuckle and 26 large cob nut bushes.

As elsewhere, a decline in fruit growing set in from the 1970s. Cheap foreign imports and more profitable uses for the land occupied by orchards—for cereal growing or housing—coupled with the steady decline in the number of small agricultural producers, all led to the virtual disappearance of orchards from the centre and south of the county during the subsequent three decades. The industry was also badly affected by the demise of the Chivers factory in Histon. In the post-war years the company suffered from a lack of investment, and in 1959 it was sold to Schweppes, who merged production with other similar companies which they had acquired, including Hartleys, the jam maker based in the north of England whom we have already met in Bedfordshire (although the Chivers family bought back most of the associated farms in 1960 and continued to grow and sell fruit, as well as continuing their dairy business). In 1986 the old factory was demolished and its site partly developed as a business park. It was replaced with a new works, costing £5 million, by new owners Premier Foods. Jam was still manufactured, but now under the Hartley brand, and alongside such products as Gale's honey, Sun-Pat peanut butter and Smash instant potato (originally developed and sold by Chivers during the Second World War as 'Pom')! The factory has since changed hands a number of times and any association with the Chivers family, or with local fruit production, has been lost. Yet while most of the orchards in the centre and south may have gone, those on the silt fens in the far north, like those in the adjacent areas of west Norfolk, have often survived. The area around Wisbech now represents one of the main fruit-producing districts in the UK, although many of the orchards are now run on more intensive lines, less friendly to wildlife, than those of earlier ages (Figure 7.4).

7.4 A typical example of a modern commercial orchard in Wisbech St Mary, north Cambridgeshire. The apples are grown on dwarfing rootstocks and will be replaced before they attain any great age; the ground around the trees is sprayed with herbicide.

A number of apple varieties originated in, or are closely associated with, Cambridgeshire. Several first arose in the gardens of large houses, such as the dessert apples Lord Peckover, which was first grown at Peckover House in Wisbech, and St Everard, which was raised in the gardens of Papworth Everard Hall. Some were developed by local nurserymen, or by the Chivers company— such as Histon Favourite, from the 1860s, or Chivers Delight, from c.1920. Others have uncertain origins, arising in the main orchard villages of the county before 1800, such as Jolly Miller, closely associated with Cottenham and probably named after a public house there. But the list of Cambridgeshire apple varieties is rather a short one, perhaps reflecting the absence of any very large nursery company in the county, comparable to Laxton's in Bedfordshire or Rivers' in Hertfordshire. More surprising, given their prominence in Cambridgeshire orchards, is the small number of plum varieties associated with the county. The Cambridge Gage and the Willingham Gage, both of which had appeared by 1800, are the only really 'traditional' examples, although Wallis Wonder (a Victoria and Severn Cross cross), a late season plum, was developed in the 1960s by Simpson's nurseries in Fordham for Mr Wallis at Heath Fruit Farm, Bluntisham. But for the most part, the extensive commercial orchards of the county were mainly, by the middle of the nineteenth century, growing varieties of fruit which had been developed elsewhere, particularly Bramley's Seedling.

There are a number of old orchards in the county which are well worth visiting. The wonderful example at Girton College in Cambridge, discussed above, can be viewed by prior appointment, while that at Rummer's Lane in Wisbech St Mary can be enjoyed from a network of permissive paths. With its huge old trees (especially Bramley's Seedlings), and its wealth of wildlife, it is hard to believe that it was only planted a century ago (Figure 7.5). It is a stunning example of an old Fenland orchard. Also of interest is the orchard at Wandlebury Country Park, a few kilometres to the south-west of Cambridge. Partly comprising old and partly more recent trees, it lies just outside the unusual polygonal walled garden which occupies the interior of an Iron Age hillfort. It was originally part of the grounds of Wandlebury House, demolished in the 1950s. In addition, a number of community orchards flourish in Cambridgeshire, including those in Trumpington (which holds an annual wassail), Histon and Impington, and Little Downham. Coton Countryside Reserve, restored by Cambridge Past,

7.5 The orchard at Rummers Lane, Wisbech St Mary, was planted around a century ago and is now a haven for wildlife.

Present and Future (CPPF), includes several orchards, planted in recent years. A heritage orchard, planted over the last two decades at Fen Edge Farm in Cottenham, hosts regular gleaning sessions (organised through Transition Cambridge). Lastly, the Orchard Tearoom in Grantchester is also worth a visit: here tea is enjoyed (wasps permitting) sitting in deckchairs in the orchard, which features quince and medlar as well as the more usual orchard fruit.

One interesting curiosity of the county is Isaac Newton's Apple Tree, which can be found growing outside Trinity College in Cambridge. Another example can be found in Cambridge Botanic Gardens. The original tree (a variety called Flower of Kent) grew at Woolsthorpe Manor in Lincolnshire, where a third example can be found. Newton was visiting his mother during a period of plague in Cambridge when the apple is said to have fallen on his head, leading him to develop his theory of gravity.

Three main commercial orchards remain in the county which market their fruit—including many heritage varieties—to the public. Heath Fruit Farm of Bluntisham sells at the farm itself, and also at the Ely and St Ives Farmers Markets; Mannings of Willingham sell in their Bushel Box farm shop; and Cam Valley of Meldreth in their local shop, and widely in Cambridgeshire and neighbouring counties at Farmers' Markets and Apple Days.

Recipes

The following two recipes are from *The Court and Kitchen of Elizabeth Commonly called Joan Cromwell, the Wife of the late Usurper, Truly Described and Represented, And now Made Public for general Satisfaction.* This volume was not actually written by Mrs Cromwell, but was instead a seventeenth-century satirical pamphlet written to discredit her—and through her, Oliver Cromwell himself. Cromwell is a man with strong local connections. He was born in Huntingdon and lived with his family in Ely for more than ten years from 1636.

Salad of Cold Hen or Pullet

Take a hen and roast it, let it be cold, carve up the legs, take the flesh and mince it small, shred a lemon, a little parsley and onions, an apple, a little pepper and salt with oil and vinegar, garnish the dish with the bones and lemon peel and so serve it.

This makes a refreshing starter. It can be made with ready-cooked chicken breast. Use finely chopped lemon flesh and spring or salad onions. The best apple to use is a Cox-type variety, that is, a dessert apple of firm texture and with some acidity. Use the apple unpeeled. Garnish with strips of lemon peel, preferably using a canelle knife, and sprigs of curly parsley. Using chicken bones

7.6 A 'salad of cold hen', a modern version of the recipe given in Court and Kitchen of Elizabeth Commonly called Joan Cromwell.

as a garnish is possibly not, perhaps, to modern taste!

ഇ✄

To Make Green Sauce

Take a handful, or a greater quantity of sorrel, beat it in a mortar with pippins pared and quartered, add thereto a little vinegar and sugar, put it into saucers. Otherwise take sorrel, beat it and stamp it well in a mortar, squeeze out the juice of it, put thereto a little vinegar, sugar and two hard eggs minced small, a little butter and grated nutmeg, set this upon the coals till it is hot, and pour it into the dish on the sippets. This is sauce for hen or veal or bacon.

Two versions are given above; one cold, the other hot. The cold version is a sort of cross between our mint sauce and the Italian Salsa Verde. It goes very well with cold roast pork and with smoked mackerel.

ഇ✄

Chicken, Gage and Almond Salad

This and the following recipes are modern inventions using varieties of fruit developed or grown in Cambridgeshire.

As we saw earlier (in the chapter on Suffolk), the greengage obtained its English name from the Gage family of Hengrave Hall. Two varieties of gage, Cambridge Gage and Willingham Gage, are associated with Cambridgeshire.

Ingredients
Cooked chicken breasts, cut into cubes

Cambridge Gages (or, if unavailable, other gage varieties, such as Purple Gage, also known as Reine Claude Violette), stoned and cut into quarters

Salad onions, chopped

7.7 Chicken, Gage and Almond Salad. The Cambridge Gage is ideal for this recipe, although other varieties such as Purple Gage can be used.

Blanched whole almonds

Mint, chopped (apple mint works particularly well as it is less strident than some other varieties)

Flat-leaf parsley

Little Gem or similar salad leaves

Dressing:
Olive oil

White balsamic condiment (less sharp than vinegar, although white wine vinegar, preferably Aspall's, could also be used)

Salt, preferably Maldon

Freshly ground black pepper

Wholegrain mustard

Garlic

Method
Make the dressing first. Place a crushed clove of garlic and a little salt and pepper into a screw-top jar. Add a heaped teaspoon of wholegrain mustard; about 4 tbsps of olive oil; and about 1.5 tbsps white balsamic condiment or 1 tbsp white wine vinegar. Shake the jar to combine the ingredients.

In a mixing bowl combine the chicken, gages, salad onions, almonds, mint and parsley. Add the dressing (shake the jar again, if necessary). The amount of dressing needed will depend on the quantities of the other ingredients, which it should coat rather than drench.

Mix carefully but thoroughly.

Place a ring of salad leaves on a serving plate or in a shallow dish. Arrange the chicken salad in the middle of the ring of salad leaves. Garnish with a sprig of mint.

This dish can be served with a herby rice salad.

This is, once again, a flexible recipe. It can be made with any variety of plum (including those with a less delicate flavour than the greengage); it can then take more robust flavourings, such as pomegranate molasses rather than the white balsamic condiment or white wine vinegar. Fresh pomegranate seeds can then be added, with pistachios instead of almonds and coriander leaf instead of flat-leaf parsley.

Caramelised Apples (serves 6)

Ingredients

6 Chivers Delight apples. If unavailable, choose a dessert variety which will hold its shape when cooked, preferably one with a colourful skin

50 g / 2 oz unsalted butter

4 tbsps Cider Brandy or 'The Somerset Pomona' aperitif

1 tbsp (or to taste) dark muscovado sugar

Method

Prepare the apples immediately before cooking. Do not peel them. Cut them into quarters, remove the core and then cut each quarter into three.

Melt the butter in a large heavy-based frying pan. Add the apple slices and cook over a medium heat, turning from time to time, until golden brown and tender when tested with the point of a sharp knife.

Place the apple slices on warmed individual plates or a serving dish.

Pour the brandy or aperitif into the pan to deglaze it, then add the sugar. Let it bubble briefly and pour over the apple slices.

Serve immediately with Greek yoghurt or good vanilla ice cream.

For use as a garnish for roast pork or feathered game, omit the sugar.

Chivers Delight or similar apples can also be roasted whole alongside pork or feathered game. Core but do not peel. Score a line horizontally around the apples with a sharp knife. Roast for around half an hour (precise timing will depend on oven temperature and size and ripeness of the apples).

಼ಂಧ

Beetroot and Bramley Apple Soup

As previously described, the Bramley's Seeding originated outside our region in Southwell in Nottinghamshire, but it became the principal variety grown in the Fens around Wisbech in Cambridgeshire and in the neighbouring parts of Norfolk.

Ingredients

25 g / 1 oz butter

1 kg/ 2 lb raw beetroot

1 medium-sized Bramley apple (the best apple to use for two reasons:

7.8 Beetroot and Bramley Soup: an innovative way of using England's most popular cooking apple, grown in the Fen orchards for nearly a century and a half.

it cooks down to purée very easily; and it has the sharpness needed to counteract the sweetness of the beetroot)

1 medium onion, roughly chopped

1 medium floury potato such as Maris Piper or King Edward, roughly diced

1 litre / 1 ¾ pints water

Salt and freshly ground black pepper

Optional: double cream and chopped chives, to serve

Method
Clean the beetroot gently, taking care not to puncture the skin (beetroot bleeds when cut). Place in a pan and cover with water.

Boil until the skin wrinkles and slips off easily (this should take about an hour but this will depend on the size of the beetroot). Discard the cooking water.

Chop the peeled beetroot roughly.

Melt the butter in a heavy-based saucepan, add the chopped onion and potato and stir to coat. Add salt and pepper, and sweat over a low heat, stirring to prevent sticking or burning.

Add the water and bring to the boil. Simmer until the onion and potato are almost tender.

In the meantime, peel, core and chop the apple. Add the apple and beetroot and continue simmering until the beetroot is tender and the apple has collapsed.

Remove from the heat and blend with a stick blender.

If the soup is too thick for your taste, add more water and reheat briefly. If the soup is too thin, boil it rapidly to reduce and thicken it. Check and adjust the seasoning.

The soup is the most glorious fuchsia colour, and looks amazing served with a swirl of double cream and sprinkled with chopped chives. The sharpness of the Bramley apple goes particularly well with the sweetness of the root vegetables. Other soup combinations that work well are Celeriac and Bramley; Curried Parsnip and Bramley (use curry paste); and Squash, Bramley and Ginger (use fresh peeled ginger root and remove it before blending). Use the same method as described above, adding longer-cooking vegetables to the onion and potato at the start.

ഇരു

Plum Crumble

This can be made using any variety of plum, or indeed a mixture. This recipe uses Wallis Wonder plums (see above), but the photograph shows a version made with Early Rivers.

Ingredients
1 lb /454 g Wallis Wonder plums

5 oz / 145 g soft light brown sugar (or to taste)

½ tsp ground cinnamon

Topping:
4 oz / 110 g wholemeal flour

2 oz / 60 g plain white flour

3 oz / 85 g butter

3 oz / 85 g demerara sugar

2 tbsps rolled or porridge oats, or chopped blanched almonds

½ tsp ground cinnamon

Method

Preheat the oven to 180°C / Gas Mark 4.

Wash, halve and stone the plums. Arrange them in a deep ovenproof dish, layered with the sugar and cinnamon.

Make the crumble topping. Sift the flours together with the cinnamon. Cut the butter into small pieces and rub into the flour. Mix with your fingertips to the 'beadcrumb' stage. Stir in the sugar and oats or chopped almonds.

Spoon the topping over the fruit.

Cook until the topping is browned and the fruit is cooked through (test with a skewer, approx. 40 minutes or so).

Serve with double cream or Greek yoghurt.

This crumble recipe can also be used for any fruit. The flavourings and type of sugar used can be varied, although using demerara for the topping does give a crunchy texture.

7.9 Plum Crumble. This can be made with a range of plums, including Wallis Wonder or, as here, Early Rivers Plums.

Further Information

We hope you have enjoyed reading this book as much as we have enjoyed writing it. We also hope that it has encouraged you to seek out different heritage varieties and to cook, eat and enjoy them in a range of dishes, both sweet and savoury. The eastern counties have a particularly rich orchard heritage as our climate has, thus far, provided excellent growing conditions for a range of fruits and nuts. As we have emphasised, since the 1970s there has been a steep decline in our orchards but recent years have seen some reversal of this trend, with the establishment of new community orchards and private collections of heritage fruit. There has also been a more general resurgence of interest in heritage fruit varieties, manifested in particular in the 'Apple Days' (and more recently, 'Plum Days') which are now regularly held around the region, and indeed nationally, each autumn. These feature a variety of activities including fruit identification and tastings, and provide an opportunity to buy interesting heritage varieties otherwise often difficult to source. It seems fitting that this book should go to press in the year that sees the 30th anniversary of the first Apple Day, which was organised by the conservation body Common Ground and held, appropriately enough, in the Old Apple Market in Covent Garden, on October 21st 1990. A list of fruit and nut events, including Apple Days, wassails and pruning and grafting courses can be found on the Orchard Network / People's Trust for Endangered Species website ----- https://ptes.org/campaigns/traditional-orchard-project/orchard-network. The website also has county lists of where trees and fruit can be bought, along with interesting orchards to visit. Further information on events and activities—and about fruit and orchards more generally in eastern England—can be obtained from the website of the East of England Apples and Orchards Project, http://www.applesandorchards.org.uk.

If this short volume has fired your interest in historic fruit, then *The Story of the Apple* by Barrie E. Juniper and David J. Mabberley (Timber Press, 2006) provides a good starting place. There are many books on apple varieties and how to identify them. Joan Morgan and Alison Richards' excellent *The New Book of Apples* (revised edition, Ebury Press 2002) is the definitive account but the beginner may prefer to start with Rosie Sanders' beautifully illustrated *The Apple Book* (Frances Lincoln, 2010); or, perhaps best of all given the author's long association with the fine orchard at Tewin in Hertfordshire, Michael Clark's *Apples: a Field Guide* (Tewin Orchard, 2015). Increasingly, however, books are being rendered obsolete as a method of identification by the wonderful website *FruitID* (www.fruitid.com). This contains a wealth of photographs, identification and tasting notes, and historical information relating to many hundreds of apple varieties and, increasingly, other kinds of fruit—pears, cobnuts and plums. Less has been published on these other kinds of fruit than on apples, but see in particular *The Book of Pears* by Joan Morgan (Ebury Press, 2015) and Margaret Roberts' *The Original Warden Pear* (Eventispress, revised edition 2018).

Only one book has so far been published on the history of an individual nursery in the eastern counties, Elizabeth Waugh's *Rivers Nursery of Sawbridgeworth: The Art of Practical Pomology* (Rockingham Press, 2009). No full history as ever been written of Lane's, Notcutts or Laxton's although for the latter see Bob Ricketts, 'The Laxtons in Bedford (1879-1957)', *Bedford Architectural Archaeological & Local History Society, Newsletter 82* (October 2008), pp.14-28, and http://virtual-library.culturalservices.net/webingres/bedfordshire/vlib/0.digitised_resources/high_street_history_laxton.htm. The only individual orchard in the region for which a history appears to have been written is Stone's at Croxley Green: see Margaret Pomfret (ed.), *Stone's Orchard, Croxley Green* (Croxley Green Parish Council, available online at www.croxleygreen-pc.gov.uk/images/downloads/StonesOrchardBooklet.pdf. Some useful information on the cultivation of fruit in the grounds of great houses can be found in *The Country House Kitchen Garden 1600—1950* Ed by C. Anne Wilson (Sutton Publishing in association with The National Trust 1998). For the fascinating story of the Coxes Orange Pippin Orchards, see A.Crossley, *The History of the Coxes Orange Pippin Orchards ("COPO") at Cockayne Hatley, 1929—1946* (Cockayne Hatley, 1999).

There is now quite an extensive literature on food history. Of particular interest are: *The Art of Dining: A History of Cooking and Eating* by Sara Paston-Williams (The National Trust 1993); *Food and drink in Britain* by C. Anne Wilson (Legend, 1973); *Cooking and Dining in Medieval England* by Peter Brears (Prospect Books 2008), and the same author's *Cooking and Dining in Tudor and Early Stuart England* (Prospect Books 2015); *Food in England* by Dorothy Hartley (Piatkus 2009); and *Traditional Foods of Britain: An Inventory*, by Laura Mason with Catherine Brown (Prospect Books 1999). Of particular relevance to the eastern counties are *Fruitful Endeavours: The 16th-Century Household Secrets of Catherine Tollemache at Helmingham Hall* by Moira Coleman (Phillimore 2012), and *East Anglian Recipes: 300 Years of Housewife's Choice* by Mary Norwak (East Anglian Magazine 1978). A welcome recent addition to the literature, and one with particular relevance to the subject of this book, is *Damsons: An Ancient Fruit in the Modern Kitchen* by Sarah Conrad Gothie (Prospect Books, 2018).

Illustrations